D0345083

MARY BAKER EDDY:
HER MISSION AND TRIUMPH

MARY BAKER EDDY

Reproduced from a crayon drawing by Elizabeth S. Eaton

MARY BAKER EDDY:

HER MISSION AND TRIUMPH

by

Julia Michael Johnston

The Christian Science Publishing Society

Boston, Massachusetts, U. S. A.

PRINTED IN U. S. A.

"Mere historic incidents and personal events are frivolous and of no moment, unless they illustrate the ethics of Truth" (Retrospection and Introspection, p. 21).

MARY BAKER EDDY

FOREWORD

This book has one purpose—to bring into focus for the reader something more than chronology can reveal of a character. The thoughts of Mary Baker Eddy are the substance of her life story. They ripened into action, led to discovery, and garnered spiritual treasure for the world. Not merely a woman of New England, nor of her century, Mrs. Eddy's history is found in her inspired published convictions and their continuing sequence of healing and redemption for humanity.

J. M. J.

CONTENTS

I

Spiritual Revival

THE latter half of the nineteenth century in New England was pre-eminently a time of mental discovery. A great intellectual upheaval was stirring beneath the surface of everyday existence in preparation for a new spiritual order. Wherever the crust of human misconceptions was thinnest, wherever thought was least fettered by materialistic dogma, there the deep-sprung impetus was felt and perception rose into greater freedom.

Newborn ideas crowded to the fore in press and pulpit. Some of these were to grow in favor after mighty wrestlings with established beliefs. Their spiritual rationality enabled them to survive opposition and bring forth sturdy evidence of their more-than-human origin. The eagerness with which new ideas were discussed encouraged freer thinking. From uplands of rarefied thought broader horizons were revealed from which there could be no returning. Mounting visions incited the forthright thinkers of these days to further comprehension of things unseen. They trod unfamiliar paths of thought through thickets of traditional doctrine, but their rugged reasoning and idealism impelled progress. One of the mental pioneers of these times wrote:

> God spoke to me while I walked the fields. I read not the Gospel of Wisdom from books written by man, but from the page inscribed by the finger of God. (The Journals of Bronson Alcott, edited by Odell Shepard, p. 133.)

New England was blessed during this era with literature of native vigor and common sense, with delightful phrasing of romance and realism, with intuitive writing and stimulating sermons. The atmosphere of untrammeled thought was conducive to broader vision, to the elevation of human consciousness to spiritual revelation. A season was at hand propitious for the fulfillment of the promise that "the Spirit of truth" would come to men and guide "into all truth." This fulfillment came in the reappearing of Christianity in its primitive strength of the first centuries when the sick as well as the sinning were healed by divine means, and the raising of the dead, in the words of Gibbon, "was very far from being esteemed an uncommon event" (The History of the Decline and Fall of the Roman Empire, by Edward Gibbon). Furthermore there was to be revealed the Science of such healing.

The voice of truth's revival was not heard in the thundering oratory, lofty erudition, or speculative mysticism of the times. As of old it was the "still small voice" of revelation speaking through the inspired Word of the Bible. This revival of "the Word . . . made flesh," Truth known by its effect among men, came not where religious orthodoxy's crimson carpet waited for a royal guest, but where a humble heart was hungering and thirsting for the lost element of Christian healing. To a woman meek in spirit, strong in faith, persistent in hope, the new revelation of Spirit came. This woman was the Discoverer and Founder of Christian Science.

Mary Baker Eddy thought in a time of mental prodigies, wrote in an age of literary masters, and healed spiritually in a period of marked medical research. At the outset she was the least influential, whereas today the importance of her discovery is patent to millions. The blessings of the revelation of Truth to her consciousness are sweeping the globe in an ever-swelling tide.

Hers was a pilgrimage in spiritual perception. She found the element of Christian healing because she sought for it as men quest for buried treasure. Her great adventure attained its goal of discovery only after years of patience, persistence, and sacrifice. In and out among the labyrinths of mundane philosophies, up and down through the intricacies of human relationships, her sacred enterprise persisted. Assurance at times sped her progress; at other times she seemed caught in the whirlpool of outward events. But ever the God-inspired undertaking went forward. Always in full view of her critics, yet ever under divine protection, she journeyed on. Daring for a world her incentive never lagged. Impelled by intuitive conviction she explored the realm of the unseen and opened a highway of spiritual progress for posterity.

New England gave Mary Baker Eddy her birthplace, and counts her among its eminent offspring. But hers was a greater heritage than any land could bestow, something out of the infinite that did its will with her and claimed her for its own.

II

First Signs of Christian Healing

IN the year 1821 the world at large was unaware of the cluster of farmsteads called Bow on the edge of the Merrimack River in New Hampshire. But the descendant of seven generations of Bakers on the Western continent, the babe born there on the sixteenth day of July, was to transform a world's thinking. This child was to add to the annals of her family a record of rarest achievement. She was to contribute to the history of the human race a deep and permanent spiritual momentum.

As the tide of mental revolution in New England touched the countryside of Bow it speeded preparation for important undertakings in the life of Mary Baker. Perhaps the first step toward her momentous discovery was taken when she was twelve years of age. Of itself the circumstance was inconsequential, yet in the light of future events it proved to be of vital significance. Mary's confidence in the loving nature of God was openly challenged by her father at the time of her examination for church membership. He ex-

of religious faith. It was as natural for her to do this as to breathe.

One day during her attendance at the Sanbornton Academy an escaped inmate of a near-by insane asylum entered the schoolyard. The frightened students fled into the schoolhouse; all but Mary. She went straight up to the man and, taking him by the hand, led him to the gate and he went quietly away. Whether or not Mary Baker then realized it, she had been given another proof of the vitality of Christian healing.

The childhood period of development preparatory for more definite phases of the great undertaking unfolded quietly through busy days of home life and school hours. The delicate health with which Mary Baker struggled during her girlhood finally necessitated her withdrawal from the country school which her sisters and brothers attended. This move may have freed, instead of hindered, her education. In her studies at home she could progress in proportion to her uncommon ability to learn, instead of conforming to the necessarily slower curriculum of the school. There she pursued her favorite subjects of moral science, logic, and natural philosophy.

Odell Shepard, in his "Pedlar's Progress" (p. 14), telling of the boyhood education of Bronson Alcott, not an unusual one for those times, writes:

Finally, and best of all, there was the family, the home—in short, one's mother. All these things, taken together, would constitute a school, and it would go hard if one did not get an education out of them. . . . Was not his mother a far wiser, kinder, gentler, and in every way better person than the school mistress? And what could that mean, unless that there are more important things in the world than reading, writing, and the exact knowledge of the length of the Zambezi River? His mother knew things too, although one never found them set down in books, and even she seldom tried to say them in words. She said them in the way she acted, in the touch of her hand; in the smile of her eyes; and often she seemed to be saying them when sitting quietly beside him, paring apples or mending a hole in his homespun coat.

While from the first responding to the influence of the best literature Mary Baker did not use the words of others as the reservoir for her wisdom, but rather as an incentive to original and inspired thinking. In early years her thought found expression in poetry which was as gentle and graceful as the swishing of silken skirts. But, later, there was the sound of portentous footsteps in her writing, the measured tread of one who moves with purpose, the strength of him who goes to war, the swiftness of a messenger who bears great tidings, the majesty of an ambassador for Christ.

Among Mary's brothers and sisters, Albert was her favorite and an exceptionally close bond existed between them. When he was home from Dartmouth College they spent happy hours together, while he instructed her in Hebrew, Greek, and Latin. Her admiration for his scholarly attainments was intense, and keen was his appreciation of her eager efforts to acquire learning.

There were other essential lessons not in books to be gained for the journey ahead. Until Mary was fifteen years of age the farmstead at Bow formed her environment. There lived three generations. In this New England farmhouse with its broad acres sloping toward the Merrimack, maturity and youth combined their industry and interests.

There was work for all, but the physical labor essential to maintain a productive farm did not interfere with generous hospitality, political interests, and, above all, deep religious experience. The Bible was the central life of the family. Mary heard its stories at her grandmother's knee. Her mother was regarded as deeply spiritual, one who wove the woof of Biblical truth into the warp of daily tasks. Her father, for a time chaplain of the State Militia, combined parental authority with Calvinistic doctrines.

Many seeking advice, including ministers, politicians, neighbors, and strangers, crossed the threshold of this home. They were welcomed with courtesy, refreshed with gracious hospitality, and entertained with culture.

It was not the custom in the home life to segregate different ages. Youngsters were not sent away when visitors came, nor was grandmother banished to her room when the children received their friends. Consideration, unselfishness, and interchange of thought flourished in the communal spirit which prevailed.

In the glow of evening firelight the education of the children was enriched by wholesome views expressed by the hard-working and strong-thinking father. To these were added stimulating memories rehearsed by the grandparent, and the mother's gentle, spiritual persuasions. Her youthful years amid such environment prompted Mary Baker to say to members of her own household in later years, "Home is not a place. It is a power."

III

Seeking Divine Science

T was from such a stimulating atmosphere that Mary Baker's girlhood, rich with quiet sweetness, budding with literary talent, and balanced by practical knowledge of home and social affairs, was to emerge into womanhood. Two people who thought highly of this young girl's literary and spiritual qualities contributed to her development during this period. They were Professor Dyer H. Sanborn, whose private school she attended, and the Reverend Enoch Corser, a Calvinistic pastor. The clergyman once praised her, as a young girl under his tutelage, in no uncertain terms. "Bright, good, and pure, aye brilliant! I never before had a pupil with such depth and independence of thought. She has some great future, mark that. She is an intellectual and spiritual genius." To her he said, "Mary, your poetry goes beyond my theology" (The Life of Mary Baker Eddy, by Sibyl Wilbur, p. 33). This was the second time in her experience that dogma had bowed before spiritual intuition.

With her emergence into womanhood Mary Baker

was to face both intense sorrow and joy, the former in advance of the latter. Her dearly loved brother and companion, Albert, the student of abstract metaphysics with whom she could speak of her deepest desires and convictions, passed on. It was good that joy followed soon after this experience, gently erasing the deeper imprints of grief and opening a path to new duties and pleasures. George Washington Glover, a friend of another brother, came to visit in the Baker home and fell deeply in love with Mary. Two years after the passing of Albert they were married and went to live in Charleston, South Carolina.

Thus in the winter of 1843 Mary Baker Glover left New England for the sunny Southland. Instead of New Hampshire's ice-bound lakes and snowy hills, the tidal basin of the Ashley and Cooper Rivers surrounded her new home. Southern dignity and leisure evidenced wealth accumulated from rice and cotton plantations spread along the reaches of the rivers. Stately mansions guarded their privacy with high, wrought-iron gates. But gatherings within their sumptuous drawing rooms were not immune to widespread murmurings of social unrest.

As Mary Glover and her husband drove through vistas of Charleston streets shaded by great oaks, she may not have heard human cries of anguish coming from whipping posts in the slave quarters. But she was not lulled into apathy by the charm of her surroundings.

It was evident that the city's wealth resulted largely from unpaid labor. George Glover agreed with his bride about the wrong of slavery, but seemed helpless to act according to his convictions. He had been forced to accept slaves in payment of debts, and a statute in 1820 had made it hard in South Carolina for an owner to free them.

Just as the political strain made it difficult for him in his daily affairs, so the way could not always have been easy for Mrs. Glover in her new surroundings. Her father, a Northern Democrat, was not in active sympathy with abolition. Her husband's business relations were with those who opposed abolition. In the North she had heard many discussions of this burning subject, but it was a very different matter to hold strong convictions against slavery in the South. Her protests against this great evil gradually found expression in letters to the press under a pen name.

With Mary Glover conviction demanded expression. Loyalty to an ideal meant more to her than approbation. It never occurred to her to surrender her ideal when challenged by custom.

The necessity for a business trip interrupted the

home routine of the Glovers. They went to Wilmington in North Carolina, intending to stay some time. Four months after their arrival George Glover was stricken with yellow fever. Because his wife was soon to become a mother she was not allowed to be with him. Accustomed to meeting adverse circumstances by resort to prayer, she spent the waiting hours in hopeful trust. But on the ninth day of his illness Major Glover passed on.

Now the way led back to her father's home. Far from being a retracing of footsteps, this was a move toward the goal. Her path was to lead upward despite devious windings until new peaks of thought were to come into view, pointing the path of discovery in the years ahead.

Major Glover's friends and brother Masons helped the young widow to settle her affairs in Charleston and to return to the parental arms outstretched to receive her. With her father's consent she informally freed her slaves. This left her with only the modest sum which she had brought from her Southern home.

Less than two months after her return a son was born to this physically frail, yet spiritually strong, mother. Her family despaired of her life and the flame of her endeavor almost went out. But this was not to be. There came hope to sustain her through months of helplessness, patience to endure through times of dependence, and courage for the coming years. Divine purpose mended the broken heart, rekindled the will to work, and established the hesitant footsteps.

All the love of the household, which now included father, mother, and one brother, was poured out to the invalid. Everything centered about her needs and by slow degrees she once again took her place in the family circle. The joyous moment came when her babe, who had been tenderly cared for by others during her illness, was brought back to her. But his health and vigor proved too much for her frailty. Again he had to be entrusted to those who had nursed him.

As she grew stronger day by day Mary Glover could not help sensing a change in her mother, and while the rest of the family were occupied with business and social affairs Mary remained much at home. Prior to Mary's birth Mrs. Baker had devoted much time to inspired prayer and Bible study. Now these two who had faced the beginning of human life together were thinking beyond its end. Of what they talked we may not know, nor of the deep affection expressed by them during those days. But the victory of spiritual faith must have been with them both when the parting came.

One blow after another had fallen until this gentle woman was deprived of husband, mother, of health, support, and the comfort of her child. At the end of another year, when her father remarried, she went to live a dependent in her sister's house. There was no place there for her own son, and for several years she was to see around her the unfolding of happy married life, with all that had been denied to her. She was to feel the mental domination of her sister, and the need of guarding her own convictions. Continuing illness prevented her from active participation in the vigorous movements of human society thronging these years. Here was a situation which called for more than New England pluck. Her Christian qualities overcame the human weakness, and she went forward in her pursuit of true healing, healing of heart and mind, as well as of body.

During the three years that Mrs. Glover lived with her sister she sometimes taught in the Sunday school and frequently wrote for newspapers and periodicals. She occasionally substituted as teacher in the reorganized Academy and opened an infants' school of her own. This enterprise did not succeed, however, for her method of teaching was not strict enough for the New England thought of that time.

The most significant event of this transitional period was her investigation of homeopathy. With this step the course of her seeking began to take shape. From then on, instead of chancing upon infrequent signs of final achievement, she was to pursue explorations which would steadily lead to the fulfillment of her search for spiritual healing.

When about eighteen years of age, Mary Baker had first tried homeopathy as a means of healing, a cousin having treated her. She had found in this method relief after allopathic methods had failed to cure her. This time she determined to study homeopathy. No longer the passive patient of earlier years, she was now a keen investigator, searching for knowledge as well as healing.

This search, though disclosing interesting results, was not satisfying. She found that the same drug which disposed of symptoms also produced them. A homeopathic remedy containing not an atom of medicine changed symptoms of disease. This indicated that the faith of doctor and patient in the remedy, not the remedy itself, produced the cure. She later wrote: "Homeopathy mentalizes a drug with such repetition of thought-attenuations, that the drug becomes more like the human mind than the substratum of this so-called mind, which we call matter; and the drug's power of action is proportionately increased" (Science and Health with Key to the Scriptures, p. 157). The diminishing of the use of the drug seemed to her to be the main advantage of the system. She reasoned that it identified the method with mind and so led thought to approach the possibility of a higher healing power. In that case was it necessary, or even honest, to administer remedies?

This question puzzled her as at intervals she pursued her research in homeopathy, and even successfully treated some cases, among them one of typhoid fever and another of advanced dropsy. Her heart was longing for Christian healing, and homeopathy seemed based on the action of the human mind over matter. Nevertheless, it was a step beyond allopathy, for it took account of the patient's mental state, as well as the physical condition. Several years later she was convinced of the inability of homeopathy to meet her demands for healing. Undaunted she pressed on in her quest.

IV

Progress

HE longing for her child, and perhaps for a home of her own, had now become so strong that Mrs. Glover seemed no longer able to endure the separation. There was no possibility of her son's joining her in her sister's home, or in the house of her father. She, herself, was unable to provide support for her child. Now thirty-two years of age, Mrs. Glover was a charming woman in appearance, with fresh complexion, clear, deep-set eyes and chestnut curls. Always gracious in demeanor, becomingly dressed, and unusually intelligent, her name had been coupled with more than one suitor for her hand. Some of the members of her family strongly urged her to accept the proposal of a Dr. Patterson, a dentist of some reputation and a cousin of her step-mother. They felt that this would be the solution of the problem of regaining her boy, now nine years old. So the decision was made in Dr. Patterson's favor. He recognized that Mrs. Glover's health was affected by constant yearning for her child, and assured her sister and her father that he would unite these two. He also hoped that he might be able to restore her health by homeopathic treatments.

Mary Glover began her life as Dr. Patterson's wife in Franklin, New Hampshire. George Glover was not allowed to come to live with his mother, nor was her health improved under her husband's care. He was much away from home, his work taking him to surrounding villages. After two years of lessening business and dwindling income the Pattersons moved to North Groton in the New Hampshire hills. Here Dr. Patterson, with borrowed money, had purchased a hundred acres of land which included a good site for a sawmill. This sawmill the doctor attempted to run in addition to his dentistry, but neither venture prospered.

The new home was a lonely spot for his wife, and as woods and mountains hemmed in her home, even so discouragement seemed to bear down upon her spirit and block every effort for recovery. The sturdy folk of the locality were occupied with endless tasks of hillside farms and community interests, but the children had time to run in and out of the Patterson home and shyly make friends with the gentle lady who was seeking to regain her health.

However, there was one advantage for Mrs. Patterson in this situation; they were not far from where George was living with those who had cared for him from his birth. Now at last mother and son were able to meet. George loved to come to see her, and her heart was greatly comforted by his visits. It is unaccountable that both Dr. Patterson and the family with whom George lived became jealous of the great happiness which these two found in each other's company. They even went so far as to say that this companionship was detrimental to her health. Shortly afterward George was taken to Minnesota to live. Mother and son were not to meet again until he had come to man's estate. George was told that his mother was dead, and she was made to believe that he was lost. Search as she would she could find no trace of him.

This mother, deprived of the affection of her only child, was later to be loved by thousands whose spiritual birth sprang from her revelation of Truth.

The path of enterprise was running through a deep valley of discouragement in which the stream of hope was almost dried and no way out appeared to the weary traveler. Mrs. Patterson, now left much alone, was a great sufferer often confined to her bed under homeopathic treatment and dieting. Hers was a desperate attempt to break the fetters of disease. In proportion to her weaning from human dependence came the necessity for leaning upon the divine. The more she leaned, the more strongly she felt the support of the everlasting arms. She turned more and more to her Bible for comfort, and with this help moved slowly on through the valley.

During this period an incident occurred which kept alive the hope of finding Christian healing. A mother brought her blind baby to Mrs. Patterson and asked her to implore God to heal her child. Mrs. Patterson's heart was filled with compassion and she lifted her thought to God, the loving, omnipotent Father of all His children. The Bible promise, "Where two or three are gathered together in my name, there am I in the midst of them" (Matthew 18:20), was still vital. The child's sight was restored. This was enough to vanquish discouragement and renew endeavor. She found herself making a solemn promise to God that if He raised her up to health she would devote her life to the healing of mankind. In a memorandum dictated after the discovery of Christian Science, she recorded that she had kept her promise.

The Pattersons left North Groton and settled for two years in near-by Rumney. This was during the years 1860–1862, which marked the beginning of the Civil War. Early in 1862, Dr. Patterson secured a noncombatant commission from the Governor of New Hampshire. Captured by the enemy, he was absent from home about nine months.

In the West, Mrs. Patterson's son had enlisted, though only sixteen. He served throughout the war, was wounded at the battle of Shiloh and at the close of the war received a government appointment in Dakota Territory. While in the army he learned of his mother's whereabouts and wrote to her. What depths of emotion must have been stirred when this letter reached the lonely woman in the New Hampshire hills! The letter was not followed by a visit until George Glover was thirty-four years old and had a wife and two children.

During these days the windows of the Rumney home framed lovelier views than the prospects in Mrs. Patterson's heart. As she looked across the valley toward stately mountains, beauty and grandeur whispered courage to her struggling sense. Neither the things that had been, nor the things that were, held any promise for the future, but the hope of that unknown something which was to come, remained paramount in her consciousness.

Before Dr. Patterson left for the South he and his wife had heard of some remarkable cures accomplished by a man in Portland, Maine, known as "Dr." P. P. Quimby. His method was drugless. He was not a spiritualist, nor a religionist in any sense of the word. An unlettered man and a clockmaker by trade, he had given public exhibitions of mesmerism for several years. Discovering that he could help the sick, as he believed, he forsook the trickery of the platform for an earnest and generous endeavor to benefit the suffering. There were elements of mesmerism, later called hypnotism, in his method, because he sought humanly to control the thoughts of those who came to him for help. He finally succumbed to his own system, believing that he had taken the illness of his last patient, and could do nothing to help the man or himself. He passed on in January, 1866.

In the use of mesmerism or hypnotism, it is interesting to note that the effect produced is dependent more upon the complete consent of the subject than upon the mental state of the manipulator. It has been found that very young children cannot be controlled by this method, for they are unable consciously to give such consent.

Some considered Mr. Quimby a charlatan, but many sought his help. Among the latter were persons who believed in mental suggestion and psychic force; in other words, in methods of attempted healing by the human mind. Some of these beliefs have persisted in the development of so-called faith-healing cults. Others have faded into comparative oblivion. It is doubtful if Mr. Quimby's name would have been known to posterity had it not been for his brief association with Mrs. Patterson as his patient.

In answer to a letter from Dr. Patterson, Mr. Quimby had replied that he was sure he could cure his wife. While the Doctor was a prisoner of war in the South, Mrs. Patterson must have referred to this letter and to a tract which Mr. Quimby had sent them. Her hours of invalidism, which denied her any active part in the great drama of freedom going on in the nation, were nevertheless filled with mental energy. She was fighting a great battle, but without flags or drums. Against the army of arguments which assailed her thought, arguments of helplessness, suffering, poverty, uselessness, failure, disappointment, she was struggling, single-minded for victory.

Single-minded, for her one weapon of warfare was the ever-growing confidence that a divine Science of deliverance from disease existed to be discovered, if only she knew how and where to find it. Medical practice in various forms and religious doctrines had failed to reveal such a power. Yet, since childhood she had cherished the Scriptural promise, "And these signs shall follow them that believe; . . . they shall lay hands on the sick, and they shall recover." When she had turned to God for help, her childhood fever had yielded, the insane man at the school had become harmless, and only recently the blind baby had received sight. There was also the memory of unusual salutations which she had heard as a child, when her saintly mother had advised her to answer in the words of Samuel: "Speak, Lord; for thy servant heareth."

Perhaps with these experiences in thought, she studied the accounts of spiritual healing in the Bible. A fresh fervor took hold of her. She determined at all costs to go to Mr. Quimby in Portland, desperately hoping that she might find relief through his ministrations, and that with this relief might come the long-sought mode of divine healing.

Mrs. Patterson asked her sister to arrange the journey, but the plan met with disapproval. Instead, she was sent to a Hydropathic Institute in Hill, New Hampshire. Here she came in contact with patients of Mr. Quimby who had been benefited by his method. It was not long before she managed to go to Portland, where she found relief from her suffering after her first visit with Mr. Quimby.

This period may be regarded as the most dangerous part of the search because, coupled with her respite from pain, was the false impression that she had reached her journey's end. Because of her own great spirituality she insisted that the power that had helped her was from God, and sought its science in talks with Mr.

Quimby and through the study of his notes. Here she found no hint of anything beyond personal mesmerism. He could not teach her what he did not know. Her faith must have colored this experience with rainbow hues, which were to fade after a few months, when some of her physical difficulties returned. Again and again she questioned Mr. Quimby about his method. Strive as she would she could not find the light she sought, because it was not there. She was compelled to search further.

In later years Mrs. Patterson, then the Discoverer of Christian Science, understood and exposed the wickedness of mesmerism, its utter falsity. Through spiritual revelation she learned the Science of one infinite, divine Mind, and the consequent illusion of the baneful belief in many minds acting upon each other for good or evil.

One of her pupils in 1887, while receiving her instruction in Christian Science, wrote: "She said to-day that mesmerism was found out, it was a big bubble and had 'busted'. We had been fooled; and now she laughs about it, and she did laugh like a girl over it." (Reminiscences of Annie Rogers Michael.) Her laughter has set reverberations of joy ringing in the hearts of thousands whom her teachings have delivered from the mesmerism of sin and disease.

The year 1864 found the Pattersons reunited and established in Lynn, Massachusetts. Mrs. Patterson was in improved health though not entirely well, and the opportunity for social enjoyment was greater than she had known for some time. Yet, stronger than all else, persisted the urge of her search, though she had no hint of being close to the attainment of her heart's desire. Indeed, she seemed to have emerged from one disappointment only to enter another, for Dr. Patterson was tending toward his final desertion of her, which came three years later when this unfortunate marriage was to end in divorce.

At the age of forty-six, Mrs. Patterson found herself again alone, her father gone, her only support an annuity of two hundred dollars a year, and knowing not which way to turn. Of this time she has written, "Previously the cloud of mortal mind seemed to have a silver lining; but now it was not even fringed with light" (Retrospection and Introspection, p. 23). Had all her struggles been in vain? Were all her hopes illusions? These questions many a brave adventurer has asked himself when all seemed lost, and found his answer, as did she, in the breaking of a dawn wherein the haven lay revealed.

V

Discovery

OW aware of her divine destiny was this woman of the ages? How prescient was she of the flood of revelation which was to embrace and permeate her being? Certainly her consciousness was prepared for a holy experience though the form of this experience was as yet undefined. The circumstance which gave tangibility to the revealing of divine Truth to her thought was her healing through spiritual illumination of supposedly fatal conditions resulting from an accident.

On the first evening in February in 1866 Mrs. Patterson went out from her home in Swampscott through wintry streets to attend a temperance lecture in Lynn. Slipping on the icy sidewalk she fell, sustaining a concussion of the brain and an injury of the spine. A doctor was summoned and she was carried into a near-by house where she remained unconscious until the following morning, when with greatest care she was removed to her home. The following Sunday found her near to death. Of this experience she has written:

When apparently near the confines of mortal existence, standing already within the shadow of the death-valley, I learned these truths in divine Science: that all real being is in God, the divine Mind, and that Life, Truth, and Love are all-powerful and ever-present; that the opposite of Truth,—called error, sin, sickness, disease, death,—is the false testimony of false material sense, of mind in matter; that this false sense evolves, in belief, a subjective state of mortal mind which this same so-called mind names *matter,* thereby shutting out the true sense of Spirit.

My discovery, that erring, mortal, misnamed *mind* produces all the organism and action of the mortal body, set my thoughts to work in new channels, and led up to my demonstration of the proposition that Mind is All and matter is naught as the leading factor in Mind-science. (Science and Health, p. 108.)

Mrs. Patterson's recovery followed her request to be left alone in her room. Taking the Bible, she read in the ninth chapter of Matthew the account of Jesus' healing of the palsied man. As she read, she felt the curative touch of the eternal Christ, and she, too, arose from her bed and walked.

At last the years of waiting were over, the darkness past. The great adventure to find divine Science was merging into Truth's revealment. The moment of discovery had come, that moment which was to lengthen into years of expanding revelation.

As the individual agency for the revelation of Christian Science, Mrs. Patterson had been fitted for her part through steady spiritual unfoldment. Whereas philosophies of men had disappointed her, inspired concepts of causation brought profound satisfaction. As one by one human kinships had been found wanting, the relationship between Deity and His offspring became more real to her. In contrast with the poverty of materialism, the riches of Spirit increased. The same spiritual impulsion which ever loosened her grasp on human aid, tightened her hold on changeless Love. She was prepared to yield to the divine purpose. Of this time the Discoverer of Christian Science writes:

> I then withdrew from society about three years,—to ponder my mission, to search the Scriptures, to find the Science of Mind that should take the things of God and show them to the creature, and reveal the great curative Principle,—Deity. (Retrospection and Introspection, p. 24.)
>
> The search was sweet, calm, and buoyant with hope, not selfish nor depressing. I knew the Principle of all harmonious Mind-action to be God, and that cures were produced in primitive Christian healing by holy, uplifting faith; but I must know the Science of this healing, and I won my way to absolute conclusions through divine revelation, reason, and demonstration. (Science and Health, p. 109.)

The Bible was Mrs. Patterson's textbook. As she bent over the sacred pages she was glimpsing universal salvation from evil, listening with "fierce heart-beats" (Christ and Christmas) for divine inspiration. She heard the whole world's cry for deliverance from woe and sensed the inevitable struggle with erudite theology, "isms," and pharmacology before that cry could be fully answered through the power of Christian healing.

With eager comprehension this searcher of the infinite reached out to receive divine Science, and translated the message into language humanly comprehensible. She tells us that at first the translation was but a feeble attempt to express in writing the vision that was gradually unfolding. But the scribe never faltered, nor did the revelation fail—that revelation of spiritual being which sometimes came swiftly as a waterfall over the precipice of her thought, again quietly as a current assembling in the depths of her being.

The inspiration gleaned from her profound study of the Bible was gradually formulated and systematized, revealing the Principle and laws of eternal Life. This discovery of the laws whereby Christ Jesus and the prophets of the Old and New Testaments performed their cures and overcame the assaults of materialism can only be adjudged divine Science, for this Science demonstrates the health, harmony, and immortality of man's existence, and is found in the Scriptures from Genesis to Revelation.

Some there are who will take issue with these bold statements, and well they might, were there no proof to substantiate them. But coincident with the revelation was the demonstration of each statement. The example of the master Christian was followed by this disciple in precept and practice. In her contacts with others, healings occurred quickly, naturally, and with mathematical certainty, thus confirming the scientific aspect of the discovery.

During the three years of her withdrawal from society, the Discoverer was led ever deeper into a realm where priceless treasure of thought was revealed. Her deep desire to share these riches with the rest of the world led to the making of notes as Truth unfolded to her consciousness. Since the discovery was Science it must be exactly stated and proved through spiritual law related to human needs. Would not untold time be needed for this endeavor? How could she meet the demands of such vast enterprise?

The years between 1866 and 1875 answered these questions by forcing the roots of Mrs. Patterson's life deeper beneath the subsoil of human dependence to the basic strata of divine trust. There refreshing streams of revelation nurtured her strength and her work. For her this was a time of growth in spiritual stature and in favor with God, if not with men. Tempests of opposition neither uprooted the Discoverer's fealty to purpose nor prevented its unfoldment.

The inner urge was ever mightier than the outer storm. It mattered not to Mrs. Patterson that others were skeptical of the means by which her health had been restored. It mattered not that she lacked funds to meet her simplest needs. It mattered not that her sister offered to build her a house next to her own if she would abandon the pursuit of her ideal. The first taste of her discovery was too satisfying, the promise of the future too tremendous to exchange them for the cramped monotony of human dependence. Though it might, and did, mean continued struggle with poverty and loneliness she must persist in her investigation.

During this period of nine years, deserted by her husband, her home given up, Mrs. Patterson was a boarder in the house of one family after another in Lynn and other places. As she went on her way of spiritual discovery there was nothing to shield her from the curiosity, ridicule, and not infrequent animosity of members of these households. It was not easy to find opportunities for friendly and fruitful interchange of thought.

As the light of spiritual understanding illumined her consciousness, it progressively dispelled the darkness of human philosophies together with what she had learned from medical theories. Previous misconceptions of curative power were replaced by the scientific truth which excluded matter as either patient or remedy in the healing work. God's ability to preserve the perfection of existence became so magnified to her thought that she was able to comprehend why Christian therapeutics needed no support from drugs, surgery, or hygiene.

As explained in the textbook of Christian Science, written during this period, Christian Science healing operates to disclose man as always spiritually perfect, rather than to struggle with the imperfections of mortals. This is accomplished through the understanding and application of spiritual law, which demonstrates the falsity of discord and maintains man's primal and eternal Godlikeness.

With clarification of thought there was born to the Discoverer of Christian Science the purpose and power to help mankind through a system which would include the elements of moral and religious reform. Immediately she set about the task of convincing the world that the time had come in which to experience final deliverance from evil in every form, by exchanging in thought and practice the mortal misconceptions of God, man, and the universe for unadulterated spiritual facts about them.

What a stupendous undertaking for any individual, especially for a woman without resources or prestige, already past the middle mark of her earthly life! Only divine impulsion could bring her purpose to fulfillment. The following extract from her writings opens a window through which we glimpse her heart at this time:

> The true understanding of Christian Science Mind-healing never originated in pride, rivalry, or the deification of self. The Discoverer of this Science could tell you of timidity, of self-distrust, of friendlessness, toil, agonies, and victories under which she needed miraculous vision to sustain her, when taking the first footsteps in this Science. (Rudimental Divine Science, p. 17.)

These footsteps passed the frontiers of creed and medicine to touch choice acres of virgin truth. It is evident that spontaneity of thought never failed to respond to the beckoning of His hand.

VI

Early Impartation

HOUGH an industrial community, church spires vied with factory chimneys in seaside Lynn. The Sabbath provided the only respite for workers from long hours of drudgery. For the majority, labor in the factories began before the completion of even a meager education; but the urge for wider comprehension persisted. Puritanical teachings could not stem the surging thought and searching criticism which were increasing signs of educational and religious revival in Massachusetts after the Civil War. As elsewhere, Unitarianism, Universalism, and spiritualism were gaining adherents.

Among the workers and thinkers in the shoe factories was an expert heel-finisher, Hiram Crafts by name. He and his wife were fellow-boarders with Mrs. Patterson in the house where she was temporarily staying. This man of modest education, reaching out for knowledge of things unseen, became the first pupil of the Discoverer of Christian Science. His thought was free from conformity to a rigid creed and not steeped in philosophy. As he talked with his teacher, he must have caught in her words a note of something finer than he had known before, for he forsook spiritualistic leanings and gave his whole attention to her teachings. She instructed him from the Bible, and from some of her manuscripts which contained the first glimpses of Christian Science, not yet entirely freed from old beliefs. Thus began the period of promulgation.

Patiently, persistently, Hiram Crafts' teacher instructed him while pursuing her own Biblical research. When Mr. Crafts gave up his occupation Mrs. Patterson moved with him and his wife to another town. Here her hours were spent in putting down inspired thoughts and in explaining these statements to her pupil. After several months of preparation for the practice of Christian Science healing Mr. Crafts was successfully established in it and by this means supported his wife and himself for some time. This was no slight accomplishment in a small community where departure from accepted standards of religion and medicine was frowned upon.

Before leaving Lynn Mrs. Patterson had healed a number of cases through her understanding of divine power. Among these cases was one of bone felon, one of delirium and fever, and one of an ailment that had confined the patient to an invalid's chair for sixteen years. These conditions were healed immediately through application of divine law without material aids.

These healings were further proof to Mrs. Glover, as she now preferred to be called, that she had found the divine power so dearly sought, and that she was correctly applying its rules. As she closely watched Hiram Crafts' work and rejoiced with him in every deliverance from suffering accomplished, she became convinced of the impersonal nature of her discovery. She had gained sufficient mastery of her subject to impart what she knew to another, so that he, too, could practice Christian Science healing successfully.

The work of her first student must have been a great comfort to her, for her more cultured friends in Lynn had not understood her presentations. Perhaps they did not want the even tenor of their religious life to be disturbed. Some people considered her insane in her attempt to spread such unpopular ideas. Her conversation about her discovery often aroused antagonism, and sometimes her quick and divinely natural healings were unacknowledged.

This attitude on the part of many with whom she came in contact, coupled with an ever-growing conviction of the importance of her work, stirred a longing in Mary Glover's heart to share her thoughts with her own family, give them proof of God's power, and sense the comfort of their comprehension of her purpose.

There is an inner chamber of the heart which the kindness of kindred warms with its presence, or chills by its absence, leaving a vacuum difficult to fill. There is something inexpressibly sweeter about the approval of one's own than all the praise the world can give.

So, for the last time, she went to visit her nearest of kin. Opposition to her "goings on" still persisted in the family. They were not desirous of sharing in her undertaking. Nevertheless, while she was with them she quickly healed a niece of a diagnosed incurable condition of enteritis preceded by typhoid fever. Even this unquestionable sign of divine power did not favorably influence her relatives. Through the years following, the gulf of their indifference widened into animosity in some instances, until finally Mrs. Glover was estranged from them all.

One touch of love, however, did come to her out of the past. The message was from her stepmother:

My Own Dear Daughter,

It is a long time since I have heard one word from you. Hope you are well and enjoying the light of God's countenance and surrounded with kind friends, a good Minister, and good society. I know you must miss your own dear relatives and former friends. . . . My love to yourself and all who are kind to you. (Mary Baker Eddy: A Life Size Portrait, by Dr. Lyman P. Powell, p. 125.)

In the late sixties, soon after the trip to see her

relatives, Mrs. Glover took up her residence in Amesbury, Massachusetts. Here, as among her kindred, she met with misunderstanding, but this did not deter her in her study and writing. After one particularly trying experience she found a welcome at the Bagley home where Miss Sarah and her sister lived. The front room with its flowered tapestry carpet, melodion, and fireplace, must have given promise of a congenial atmosphere in which to add to her "copious notes of Scriptural exposition" (Science and Health, Preface, p. ix).

During the day dressmaking and shopkeeping went on in two lower-floor rooms of the small house. While needles were busy and customers came and went, the new roomer was absorbed in her work upstairs. When evening came and the busy hands of these women rested in their laps, doubtless they talked of the things of God, for Sarah became deeply interested in Mrs. Glover's approach to the Bible and accepted her elementary ideas of divine Science. Two years later, when Mrs. Glover returned to stay with her for a time, Sarah learned the rudiments of Christian Science healing and practiced them for about twenty years. Like some others who followed these early expositions of the Discoverer of Christian Science, she mixed what was given her with beliefs quite foreign to the pure teachings which she had received.

While staying in Amesbury Mrs. Glover met John Greenleaf Whittier. He was suffering from incipient pulmonary consumption. During a visit to his home the Christ-power which both he and Mrs. Glover acknowledged as ever present healed him. This healing transmuted into reality the sentiments of one of his poems:

> He stood of old, the holy Christ,
>   Amid the suffering throng,
> With whom his lightest touch sufficed
>   To make the weakest strong.
> That healing gift God gives to them
>   Who use it in His name;
> The power that filled the garment's hem
>   Is evermore the same.
>
> So shalt thou be with power endued
>   Like him who went about
> The Syrian hillsides doing good
>   And casting demons out.
> The Great Physician liveth yet
>   Thy friend and guide to be;
> The Healer by Gennesaret
>   Shall walk the rounds with thee.

(The Healer, as adapted in the Christian Science Hymnal, No. 96.)

During this period Mrs. Glover's journeyings were closely associated with homely folk and commonplace things, but her mental activity sought and found the rarefied atmosphere of Spirit. While her body had to be satisfied with frugal living, and occasionally with rooms so cold in winter that her fingers became stiff while writing, her thought soared in freedom, aglow with revelation. The companionship of holy thoughts offset the lack of understanding in those about her. Instead of being adversely affected by surroundings, she was able in a measure to permeate the atmosphere wherein she moved with maintained purity of thought and life. Self-distrust, hesitancy, and sensitiveness were overcome. Self-consciousness was outweighed by exaltation, and timidity conquered by ever-surging and more clearly defined purpose.

For Mrs. Glover the years 1866 to 1870 were a sifting time, a getting rid of old impressions and a gaining of spiritual facts. No work is so demanding as listening to the voice of God, of Spirit, Truth. No one can hear this voice unless he listens, and he cannot listen until the human self is stilled. Men have done this on mountaintops and in sanctuaries when relieved of all human responsibilities. This seeker, while advancing spiritually, was supporting herself in the midst of the hubbub of daily life, in homes filled with divergent opinions and conflicting elements.

Two of these years were spent in a home with a family of five. In the evenings Mrs. Glover laid aside her writings, and it was then that the two younger children would come to her room to play. Her brightness, gaiety, and kindness made her a delightful companion, and she completely won the heart of the daughter, Lucy. It was easy for children to love and trust this gentlewoman. Always her mother-heart felt the deepest affection for them.

Unfortunately the laughter in the upper room could not smother the sounds of contention below, where another member of the family objected to Mrs. Glover's presence. By this time she had become accustomed to intense contrasts of feeling toward herself. A remark which she made to one of the children upon leaving the home showed her growing awareness of the conflict which her discovery of the allness of God, good, must bring about as it challenged human knowledge of good and evil. Embracing the little girl she said: "You, too, will turn against me some day, Lucy" (The Life of Mary Baker Eddy, by Sibyl Wilbur, p. 177).

It is one thing to bring to the world a theory which pleases men and wins personal adoration. It is quite another thing to present to humanity a teaching which deprives people of their entrenched and cherished material beliefs. Mrs. Glover was learning "the vastness of Christian Science, the fixedness of mortal illusions, and the human hatred of Truth" (Science and Health, p. 330). But she did not hesitate. Wisdom and courage to withstand opposition and defend her work were appearing. The great changes going on in her consciousness were bringing to the fore the qualities of true selfhood.

She was passing through swift waters which swept away nonessentials but did not touch her spiritual strength. From this time on, the world was to feel the impress of her labors. Before the century closed, her teachings were to penetrate the fields of theology, medicine, and education, in this and foreign lands. Indeed, they were to bring about changes in the thoughts and lives of men more profound than any that had occurred since the birth of the Christian era.

VII

Teaching

HE spanning of the continent by railroad in 1869 typified the progressive spirit of the times. In this land of vast expanse, abundant rivers, virgin forests, with room enough and to spare for all who came to its shores, people were experiencing freedom of thought and living. While men fathered the general growth of a nation, women mothered ideas and contributed to the moral and spiritual development of the country. This was especially true of Mary Glover as she prepared for wider impartation, as well as for continued reception, of her vision of Christian Science.

The progress of her work at this point demanded pupils rather than patients, pupils more desirous of understanding than of aggrandizement. Means must be found through which her revelation could win its way through opposition to wider acceptance. This implied the immediate necessity for systematic teaching. At once she began to give thought and time to this demand. Her manner of conveying her ideas to pupils was through questions and answers. Her first writings on the new subject she entitled "The Science of Man, by Which the Sick are Healed." This pamphlet became the basis for her instructions in Christian healing.

Persistently Mrs. Glover worked with one pupil after another. She, too, was learning. Experience was teaching her that, while others might desire to know the truths unfolding in her thought, they might not be able to grasp the pure spirituality of her impartations, or adhere steadfastly to their demands as she herself was doing. She "learned that thought must be spiritualized, in order to apprehend Spirit. It must become honest, unselfish, and pure, in order to have the least understanding of God in divine Science." (Retrospection and Introspection, p. 28.)

It was evident that the sharing of her spiritual revelation must first establish the highest moral qualities in her students, and she never departed from this aspect of Christian Science. In some notes made by one of her pupils later are these words: "If we do not heal morally we had better not heal at all. Our work for the sinner is to destroy his belief of sin in our own sight." (Reminiscences of Annie Rogers Michael.)

During these early years of teaching and practice, in spite of limited funds, Mrs. Glover continued her intensive search of the Scriptures together with consistent writing. Occasionally she received room and board from her pupils, at other times payment for her spiritual labors in their behalf. She proved herself willing to darn the elbows of her dresses, and eat meagerly; but there was need for further resources with which to carry on her activities.

It became essential for her to devote more time to teaching classes, and to spend fewer hours instructing the occasional inquirer. A suitable place must be found in which to teach, and monetary assistance must be available, if necessary, for those coming to study and enter the practice of Christian Science. At first the tuition fee varied and was eventually raised to three hundred dollars, a considerable amount for those times. Not all the pupils paid for their instruction. Occasionally she assisted students financially. It was not in Mary Glover's nature to lean upon others. Rather did she rely upon the one divine source which not only supported her own progress, but made "many weary wings" (Miscellaneous Writings, p. 159) spring upward that they might reach divine altitudes and rest in the atmosphere of spiritually discerned existence.

A comfortable New England house in Lynn, under the shelter of spreading trees, was the setting in which the first class in Christian Science was taught. The lower floor was occupied by a young ladies' school. Mrs. Glover met with her pupils on the second floor.

The sessions were held in the evening, as the members of the class were workers in the factories during the daytime.

The Christian disciples of old, when they had left their toil, listened to the words of the great Teacher and found their hearts stirred within them. So must these humble folk have been touched by the instruction which poured from the lips of this revelator and reillumined the Master's sayings. Like the early Christians, they found the Word confirmed by healing power, for they were able to perform cures with the truths that they learned.

What times of spiritual refreshment those hours of communion in the upper chamber must have been! The realization of spiritual freedom and power must have replaced the cramping monotony of shop labor in the thoughts of the listeners. No doubt the zeal of their teacher kindled aspirations in the pupils to embody more of the divine nature. Courage from on high must have impelled this little band of mental pioneers as they went forth to solve the problems of life through spiritual understanding.

As far back as 1862 Mrs. Glover had seen that medical systems were not dependable and that a higher power must eventually govern all healing. Eight years later she was in a position to explain this to others. To aid her pupils at the time of instruction she made copies of her manuscript, "The Science of Man," for their use. After the class work she was thoughtful in guiding their footsteps, answering their many letters and in every way assisting their progress.

The loving patience shown by this gentlewoman to beginners of limited culture and means was boundless. Not always were they loyal to their teacher and teaching. A promising student who had accompanied her from Amesbury to Lynn, after two years of association with her, became disobedient. Disregarding her instructions he refused to stop manipulation of his patients. She, herself, had never used this method. There seemed no course to take other than to rebuke him and let him go. In after years he averred that he had never read her textbook, nor grasped the fundamental principle of that which she had so faithfully endeavored to teach him.

This, and other similar experiences, revealed the necessity of equipping her pupils with defense against mesmerism. In the Bible Mrs. Glover sought for reassurance of the allness and oneness of infinite, divine Mind, through which to confirm the unreality of the belief of many minds preying one upon another. Her search was rewarded. She gained from the life of the Master the understanding that man cannot be used by evil as an agent, or a victim, because man is forever governed by the one and only Mind, God, which "cannot be tempted with evil, neither tempteth . . . any man" (James 1:13). The infinity of good as Mind connoted the unreality of evil mentality. This truth was of invaluable assistance to her through the years to come. It enabled her in great measure to defend the expansion of her work against divergence, division, and deterioration.

The necessity for writing a textbook to take the place of personal notes and manuscripts had become apparent to Mrs. Glover. The robing of her thoughts in phrases suited to the stature of her thinking became of prime importance to her. There could be no mending of outworn medical and theological theories with mere threads of her vision. Fuller statements of Truth must be drawn from the source of her revelation and presented unadulterated to the world. So she started upon her prodigious task of composing the Christian Science textbook.

What changes the artistry of Christian Science had wrought in this woman! Traces of invalidism had vanished. Strength to work unceasingly was hers. Personal sensitiveness of earlier years had given place to poise. Firmness against opposition and misunderstanding had resulted in continuous progress of her work.

The nature of Christianity defined by the Master in the words, "The prince of this world cometh, and hath nothing in me" (John 14:30), was reappearing in this Christian disciple of the nineteenth century. The ability to endure suffering was replaced by the understanding which conquers it. She who once was wholly dependent upon others was rising to independence of all but God. She found her rest in ceaseless action, her strength in the omnipotence of divine Love, her joy in sharing her revelation. Neither obstacles nor triumphs halted her advance. Always she looked forward to further battles to be won. Slowly, steadily, the spiritual forces upon which she relied carried her onward.

In this picture there are no flying banners, yet the footsteps are buoyant as they advance in the overcoming of false theology, medical scoffing, and determined materialism. There is no beating of drums; only unheard music in the heavens times the onward tread. Her steadfast gaze is held by an unseen Presence. There is nothing about this figure to excite pity. Rather is there a radiance of inner grandeur which stirs the onlooker to murmur, "Here is a soldier of God."

VIII

Revelation Indited

N the days when Mary Baker as a tiny child was asked by her brothers and sisters what she was going to do when she grew up, she answered that she was going to write a book. Half a lifetime intervened between this pronouncement and the event, a period which proved the essence of her thought to be awareness of a mission, rather than personal ambition.

It is possible that her first attempt at composition was a record of her prayers at an early age. Learning of Daniel's habit of praying three times a day, she decided to emulate him and, by putting down in order the prayers which came to her lips, try to find if she improved in her devotions from day to day.

At the age of ten years she was wholly familiar with Lindley Murray's Grammar. The text of this book is not accompanied with illustrations, nor does it seem that this compilation of poetry, philosophy, and essays is chosen with intent to appeal to youngsters. The quotations are profound and many deductions are more suitable for the advanced scholar than for a young child.

There was formed at this time the ability to study assiduously, and to persist in thinking along religious and ethical lines. Later Mary chose her reading from the best that literature offered, developing intuitive perception and original expression in her writing.

After her healing had taken place and she began to study the Bible anew, the enlightenment flowing into her consciousness demanded this original expression. New definitions of familiar terms supplied one of the means through which her phraseology took form. Of her own wording she writes:

> God I called *immortal Mind.* That which sins, suffers, and dies, I named *mortal mind.* The physical senses, or sensuous nature, I called *error* and *shadow.* Soul I denominated *substance,* because Soul alone is truly substantial. God I characterized as individual entity, but His corporeality I denied. The real I claimed as eternal; and its antipodes, or the temporal, I described as unreal. Spirit I called the *reality;* and matter, the *unreality.* (Retrospection and Introspection, p. 25.)

From these definitions unfolded further understanding of the Science of Life and the art of presenting it to the human race. This spiritual pioneer was gaining the discernment of Truth together with the Christianly scientific method of dealing with evil. Her earliest notes state the falsity of mortality and the allness of Spirit with gradually increasing clarity.

At first, some of Mrs. Glover's readers found her

writings so original that they were difficult to understand. Members of the medical profession looked upon her as an impostor. Churchmen there were who felt that she was the emissary of the devil. Spiritualists, kinder to her than were others, claimed her as a medium. Thus, from the first, she found it necessary to state that her method was not a form of matter-medicine, hygiene, human psychology, electricity, magnetism, or mediumship. To use her own words: "I never could believe in spiritualism" (Science and Health, p. 71).

Bronson Alcott wrote in his Diary the following impression of Mrs. Glover's attitude toward spiritualism: "A former visit of mine impressed me favorably regarding her methods, and especially her faith in spiritual as distinguished from the sorceries of current spiritualism, fast running its polluting social race into detestation." (The Journals of Bronson Alcott, edited by Odell Shepard, p. 479.)

Few saw clearly what this inspired thinker beheld, or made the effort to gain her vision. She found that culture did not wish to be bothered with her "new-fangled" ideas, and ignorance responded slowly to her knocking at the door of thought. The Yankee pedlar, trudging many a weary mile to dispose of his notions, met with more response than did this New England woman, eager to share her spiritual treasures along the wayside. People were willing to experiment with patent medicines, but were not eager to possess the understanding of divine healing—the "pearl of great price." Undisturbed by scorn and indifference, she followed the promptings of her spiritual genius. From first to last, she fearlessly stated her message, buttressed it with proof, and committed it to the providence of God.

Developing perfection in her work rather than struggling against opposition, revealing spirituality instead of meddling with matter, persisting steadfastly in reception and impartation of divine ideas, after six years devoted to spiritual discovery Mary Baker Glover formulated her writings into book form. Hers was the sweetness of bitter disappointments overcome, the vision that sees beyond horizons, humility pulsating with greatness. Her aloneness was that of one whose certainty of God's leading presses on to meet the unknown.

In March, 1875, Mrs. Glover was in a position to purchase a modest home at Number 8, now 12, Broad Street, in Lynn. There was urgent need for uninterrupted quiet. But even in her own home there was not to be complete seclusion. It must have taken as much courage to arrange the manner of her living in the new quarters as it did to make this investment in real estate. While she had saved enough to buy the home, it was necessary for her to let all but two of the rooms in order to maintain it. Hours of intensive mental activity were interspersed with obligations to those about her and with the cares of a housekeeper.

Her workroom was in the upper story of the Broad Street house. Through the small skylight could be seen the only glimpse of heaven's blue. No crosscurrent of breezes cooled the room in summer, nor was it heated by diffused warmth in winter. The atmosphere of divine purpose embraced this noble woman in harmony of thought and forgetfulness of body.

The room was destitute of shelves of reference books. Not the accumulation of data, but the dawn of divine ideas, was essential to Mrs. Glover's work. It mattered little that no scholarly visitors came to stimulate endeavor. Her thinking was adventurously inspired. The light of revelation illumining the meaning of the text on the wall, "Thou shalt have no other gods before me," enabled her to complete her task.

Having fashioned the book as a "scribe under orders," Mrs. Glover set about the arduous task of proofreading, encouraged by the assurance that her book for the promulgation of Christian Science would soon reach the public with its message of Christian healing.

"Science and Health with Key to the Scriptures,"

the Christian Science textbook, as it stands today, presents the Comforter, the Christ-interpretation of the Bible. It elucidates the Science of eternal Life which the author discerned in the words and works of Christ Jesus. It is a complete statement of demonstrable religion, challenging inquiry, defining reality, outliving skepticism.

The profoundness of the book's theme evolved its own form of expression. The ruggedness of primeval truths rising from its pages causes the reader to climb the heights of holiness. He finds a vast subject accompanied by well-marked paths for investigation and proof. Here, absolute assertions combine with the power of practical application. The reader senses in the words a simultaneous letting in of spiritual illumination and a rousing to behold the eternal aurora of Spirit.

The language of the book consists of carefully chosen phrases with infinite meanings. To be understood the declarations require demonstration. Throughout the pages changeless fact and tender compassion breathe a summons to the reader to launch out into the depths of spirituality and let down his net.

The statements of Science and Health constitute a fabric of holy substance, not woven by human hand into a design to please him who peruses the pages, but unmistakably presenting the pattern of revelation. There is a sureness of expression which accompanies Science and invites proof. There is bluntness and brevity such as the master Christian used.

The reader finds that he cannot close this book and leave the words between the covers. They are a quickening animus which take root in his consciousness and begin his transformation, whether he will or not. They impel each one who understands them to discover his true sonship with God. Thus he becomes his own physician and minister. Each proof of the Science which this book contains reveals the possibility of greater works. The student of Science and Health does not come to a point of saturation in his reflection and demonstration of the truths presented by this "key" to the Scriptures, but gradually associates himself with the unfolding of eternal Truth. And who would, or can, deny Truth?

IX

Publication

HE little house on Broad Street quickly became the center of increasing activity. There was the coming and going of a growing number of pupils who often felt the necessity of carrying personal problems to their teacher. This required Mrs. Glover's time and patience —oh, such patience! Laboring mentally and physically without cessation to share her spiritual treasures with them, she encouraged their steps and assisted them in their practice, healing cases for which their understanding proved inadequate. Her love and compassion toward these early students were unbounded. Nevertheless, some of her pupils left her, and even discredited her precepts because they misunderstood her teachings. A few were practicing contrary to her instructions. All this further convinced her of the wisdom of putting her system of Mind-healing into incontrovertible form that would speak for itself.

Though this period was a trying one for Mrs. Glover, she was not diverted from her steadfast purpose. Later she wrote in a letter:

I may as well jest over the absurd striplings who turn to rend me, to threaten me with disgrace and imprisonment for giving them a discovery that money cannot pay for, but a little good breeding might have helped at least to reward the toil, and scorn, and obscurity, by which it was won for them. (Mrs. Eddy as I Knew Her in 1870, by Samuel Putnam Bancroft, p. 19.)

During these momentous days, Mrs. Glover was also teaching classes, imparting to seekers rare gleanings from the Bible. She was looking out from celestial heights, not up to them. It was difficult to persuade her pupils that their outlook could be from the same standpoint. She strove to inspire them to understand her words, and to love and live what she taught. She would not have the words of Christian Science without the works of healing. And in order to do the works the spirit of Truth must enter into the minutiae of human life.

To daily live and practice the truths she taught was the test of devotion among her followers. Those who stood the test showed their appreciation in kindly ways. Some helped to care for and beautify the new home, relieving their benefactress of minor duties. To accomplish the tasks of highest impulsion her thought needed to be inaccessible to petty disturbance and willful annoyance. It was becoming evident that her work must be protected by the same source from whence came the vision. This protection was essential, for her message ran counter to the stream of general thought, inevitably producing mental collisions and, on occasions, resistance. Some who yield to the jostling of their bodies in the crowd, instinctively stiffen against the stirring of their religious convictions.

The demands upon the strength and courage of this woman were unceasing. There were sleepless nights and weary hours. Days came when family gatherings in other homes accentuated her aloneness and her heart cried out for companionship which would hold up her hands till the long labor of the presentation of her discovery to the public should be accomplished. Yet, none but she could sense the magnitude of her revelation. No one else could write and rewrite the words which conveyed it. No one else could foresee its vast redemptive effect. Mrs. Glover presented in her textbook the wedding of Science and religion half a century before many savants and ecclesiastics awakened to this fundamental proposition.

Finally Mary Glover waited on divine wisdom for the title of her book. It was six weeks before the name "Science and Health" came to her thought. What must have been her joy when, a half year later, she was shown in Wyclif's translation of the New Testament the words "science of health," rendered "knowledge of salvation" in the Authorized Version! (Luke 1:77.)

Now that the book was nearing the time of publication many of the difficulties attendant upon its preparation were forgotten. A publisher willing to venture the printing of so unusual a manuscript had been found and the matter of financing the publishing had been solved. But further hindrance was encountered when for no apparent reason the printer delayed completion of his work. However, it was found that his unwillingness to proceed coincided with an impulsion on Mrs. Glover's part to add an essential chapter to the book. She must write all that she had discovered, and this now included a deeper comprehension of the deceptive nature of material sense, or animal magnetism, as opposed to spiritual understanding. It had been a joyous experience to write of the infinitude, the supremacy of divine Mind. It was a painful task to unmask the character of mortal mind and, through this exposure, reveal its falsity. Yet this was necessary for the full understanding of the power of Christian Science healing, which had come to deliver men from sin, disease, and death, from all thralldom to materialism. When the chapter on animal magnetism was written and taken to the printer, the publishing of the book was carried to completion.

In October, 1875, Science and Health was released from the press through W. F. Brown and Company,

50 Bromfield Street, in Boston. Here, indeed, was the fruition of that period of intensive writing which began in February, 1872, and continued until the book reached the printer in 1874. The sacred revelation which had come to Mrs. Glover's consciousness now went forth as information of profound import, a challenge to every man's faith.

Thus was launched the most momentous revolution in the history of the world's thinking since the time of the Nazarene. It set no man against his neighbor, but every man against the errors of his own thought. This mental overturning was of fundamental value, overthrowing false premises in religion, ethics, medicine, and government. It made way for the enthronement of divine reality in individual, and finally universal, human experience. It has come to bless all men. Moving forward with divine impulsion this mental revolution was, and is, resistless.

At first the book was not a "best seller." Eventually it took its place in the esteem of readers as second only to the Bible. Even in critical literary groups of New England, it received favorable comment. Among the educational leaders who noted arresting statements in Mrs. Glover's book was Bronson Alcott, founder of the Concord School of Philosophy. This original thinker was more than kindly disposed toward the new book and its author. He wrote in his Journal on January 17, 1876:

> Write to Mrs. Mary Baker Grover [Glover] of Lynn, thanking her for her remarkable volume entitled *Science and Health,* which I have read with profound interest. She purposes curing bodily disease by metaphysical methods, and teaches the soul's power over the body, its spirituality and immortality. Her book is an earnest and thoughtful appeal to the faith and reason of Christians, and will serve the ends of human culture by its appeals. I shall seek an interview with the author for comparing views on the transcendent themes discussed therein. In times like ours, so sunk in sensualism, one hails with joy any voice speaking an assured word for God and Immortality; and the joy is heightened the more if the words are of woman's divining. Mrs. Glover appears to have attained her revelations through deep physical [*sic*] experiences, and writes as a seeress of divine things. The popular Spiritualism finds no favor from her divining spirit. I cannot vouch for the details of her teachings, but am sure of her having truths to impart deserving the attention of every well-wisher of his race. (The Journals of Bronson Alcott, edited by Odell Shepard, p. 464.)

A month later Mr. Alcott, present at a meeting of Mrs. Glover and her followers in the Broad Street house, was favorably impressed with the gathering. When the press and pulpit assailed Science and Health he went to see the author, stating that he had come to comfort her. Mrs. Glover said that "his athletic mind, scholarly and serene, was the first to bedew my hope with a drop of humanity" (Pulpit and Press, p. 5).

Publication

The author's zealous pupils sold copies of her book from door to door in Boston and its environs. Those whom she had healed and taught were eager to have her exposition of Christian Science. Signs of basic changes in religious thinking followed the publication of this volume. Ridicule, annoyance, and contention were noticeable in some circles, but others accepted it as a deep draught of divine wisdom and accordingly experienced its healing power. These first reactions were the whitecaps presaging the ground swell of religious reform to follow.

X

Leadership

OPPOSITION to the radical ideas propounded in Science and Health was to be expected from the general public, but unforeseen obstruction also appeared within the group of students. Among those most closely associated with Mrs. Glover there developed petty jealousies, divergence of opinions, and personal ambitions. There was need for her to cope wisely with this difficulty, and at the same time meet the vital demands resulting from the interest aroused by the textbook. She needed a loyal and intimate helper.

In the midst of these trials there appeared one who was to prove a comfort and joy to this sorely tried woman. His was the name by which the world was to know her and millions were to love her. Asa Gilbert Eddy, of Puritan ancestry, a man of integrity with great gentleness of nature, came to her to be cured of a physical difficulty. Upon being healed he studied with her and became a devoted Christian Scientist. Mrs. Glover felt that she could love, respect, and trust Mr. Eddy. She further discerned in him qualities which bespoke helpful association for her in carrying on her great endeavor. He saw the opportunity which wedlock would give him to love and cherish Mary Glover while she continued her labor for the world. Their marriage took place on the first day of January in 1877.

At once Mrs. Eddy placed some of her responsibilities in her husband's hands. He became a successful practitioner and was the first person to use the words "Christian Scientist" on an office sign. He was of the greatest assistance to her and their companionship brought out a deep and tender unity of thought and purpose. But the Christian Science movement was under way and demanding leadership. There could be no veering from the goal set before her. Her lifework must continue to move straight as an arrow shot from the bow of omnipotence.

Her first steps toward leadership of a movement designed to free mankind from sin, disease, and death were not encouraging. The second edition of Science and Health was a failure, due to mismanagement and indifference on the part of those to whose care it was entrusted. There followed lawsuits brought by students against Mrs. Eddy and against each other. Notwithstanding two years' labor spent on the revision of the book, the workers still lacked understanding of the precepts taught therein. Nevertheless, classes continued to be held, and healings resulted from the practice of those who were sincere students. At meetings held for outsiders in a hall on Market Street, Lynn, the number of attendants had not exceeded twenty-five.

Mary Baker Eddy could hardly have been recognized as a potential world-leader during the middle seventies in New England. Yet, the Christian Science movement was not the first reform to start with a comparatively unknown individual embraced in the momentum of an all-absorbing purpose. Evidence was appearing of permanent acceptance of spiritual healing as an essential part of Christian religion. Mrs. Eddy and her followers, at first designated as "Moral Scientists," were now recognized as a religious group known as "Christian Scientists." The time had come for the inspiration and zeal quickened in individual members to be molded into collective action.

The prospect before the Christian Science Leader, if viewed from the human standpoint, seemed precarious. She was leading her followers under difficult circumstances, expecting works from them which made them targets for criticism and persecution. They could not look with certainty to the law to protect them in their use of spiritual means for physical healing. They still understood so little of what she tried to teach them that some were easily led astray. Yet with this band of neophytes Mrs. Eddy was about to inaugurate a crusade destined to liberate the human race from slavery to evil of every sort. This is shown by her statement in Science and Health (pp. 225, 226):

> The rights of man were vindicated in a single section and on the lowest plane of human life, when African slavery was abolished in our land. That was only prophetic of further steps towards the banishment of a world-wide slavery, found on higher planes of existence and under more subtle and depraving forms.

If at times her followers saw only hosts of opposing religious, medical, and materialistic believers, their Leader inspired them to understand that all having part in the unfolding venture were encompassed by "hosts of the Lord." Always aware of this support Mrs. Eddy went fearlessly forward.

This consciousness of divine power and presence equipped her for leadership and protected her followers. When discouragement assailed her, spiritual vision showed the path ahead. If despair attempted to clog her advance, it failed to stop the one who had learned to walk over, not through, troubled waters of mortal strife. Neither disaffection among her adherents, nor aggression from without, conquered her steadfast confidence in divine direction. She utterly trusted the Truth which had delivered her from frailty and suffering, from hopeless days and helpless nights, from neglect and disappointment, from loneliness and opposition, from mental groping, and finally from the last enemy. In this supreme power she recognized the Saviour of mankind.

This unique commander did not use her influence to mold the thoughts and lives of men for a selfish purpose, but led them to God's directing. "Follow your Leader only so far as she follows Christ" (Message to The Mother Church for 1901, p. 34) was her admonition. Herein lies a reason for her greatness, that greatness which was not ability to shape the world to one's own will, but willingness to yield to the shaping of the divine will. The Master of all men said of his relationship to God, "I do always those things that please him" (John 8:29).

Thus was Mrs. Eddy led by highest foresight and wisdom to guide the initial stages of a movement destined to be world-wide. Under this guidance her followers were safe and the progress of the movement was assured. Opposition lessened. Victories won brought blessings to friend and foe. More and more adherents pressed on with her to the ultimate goal: dominion over all evil, and lasting spiritual peace.

Though outward footsteps of the Discoverer and Leader of Christian Science were timed to the pace of followers, inner freedom of divine adventure was not surrendered. Her response to revelation became only more fruitful in achievement and expression.

Mrs. Eddy dealt firmly with the unrest among those close to her. She had a way of looking into a situation, through it, and far beyond it. Then she moved in accord with her farthest vision, letting the immediate circumstance fall into line with it. At times this proved very difficult for some of her followers who were mostly concerned with their personal and local sense of Christian Science. But the revelation of Christian Science had come from infinity, it moved through infinity, and the Leader moved with it.

To Mrs. Eddy the leadings of divine Mind were unmistakable. She obeyed without hesitation and achieved results. But one person could not and should not perform all the functions essential for the progress of Christian Science. Upon her rested the task of discerning the course of the movement, protecting the venturing, and providing for its expansion. Upon the students rested the obligation to present Christian Science to the community as permanent healing religion demonstrated by a united and harmonious body of workers. It was imperative for Mrs. Eddy to delegate duties to others. The time to organize more extensively was at hand.

Accepting the task of developing agencies through which to expand the mission of Christian Science she named the first organized group of six active students the "Christian Scientist Association." The previous year eight of her students had made provision for Sunday services in a rented hall on a budget of ten dollars a week. Mrs. Eddy was the pastor and director.

Increasing numbers of those desiring instruction in Christian Science and preparation for the practice of metaphysical therapeutics, demanded facilities exceeding those developed prior to the year 1881. To meet these requirements, in January of that year Mrs. Eddy organized the Massachusetts Metaphysical College. She drew "up an agreement with six students to teach pathology, ontology, therapeutics, moral science, metaphysics, and their application to the treatment of diseases" (The Life of Mary Baker Eddy, by Sibyl Wilbur, p. 262). A charter for these purposes was granted by the Commonwealth of Massachusetts. She later wrote, "No charter was granted for similar purposes after 1883" (Retrospection and Introspection, p. 43). She was the president of the college and taught most of the classes. During the seventies the Commonwealth had showed its kindly disposition towards women's advancement in the educational field by permitting the founding of Wellesley College, Smith, and Radcliffe.

The question naturally arises, How could Mrs. Eddy assume such a position without having been prepared in the generally accepted way for such curriculum? Was it colossal egotism, human will, or mad ambition that impelled this woman to take on ever-increasing responsibility, public contacts, and endless labor? Or had the divine purpose found so rare a consciousness that continuous revealment of its infinite capacities was possible? The logical sequence of ensuing events gave the answer.

An early hint of the idea of organization and its ultimate shape may be found in a remark made by Mrs. Eddy one evening in the early seventies when she and a companion returned from an unsuccessful attempt to find a publisher for Science and Health. As they passed along one of the streets of Lynn, the city where her first pupil had come to hear statements of Christian Science and where she had performed many remarkable cures, she had suddenly said: "Stop! Do you see that church? I shall have a church of my own some day." Mrs. Eddy always could see a widening horizon at the end of a lane of seeming defeat.

XI

Curative Preaching

HEN Mrs. Eddy discovered Christian Science and consecrated her life to its promulgation she did not think of herself as having left the church, but as having found the essence of religion. Christian Science came to her not as a new theory, but as the very heart of Christian teaching. It came to lift the veil of symbolism and announce the pure truth. It came to enable men in ensuing ages to do the works required of the Master's followers. Quite naturally, then, she hoped that the established churches would adopt her discovery. Though some clergymen were roused to investigate her claims, and others to open their pulpits to her, she was disappointed in her hope.

Ecclesiastical, medical, and philosophical thought, the readers who were scanning her textbook with varied emotions, began to call her to account for what she had written in Science and Health. Ideas set down on the printed page leave the shelter of the author's nursing and invite the buffeting of public analysis. The statements of Christian Science were prepared to meet scrutiny and stand on demonstration. Before many years passed, the spiritual ideas which came to Mrs. Eddy were arresting the attention of multitudes and winning their adherence.

Both the Christian Scientist Association and the Metaphysical College were to function for the benefit of those interested in Christian Science and working within the movement. The seed of Truth must find a wider field of acceptance in order to bring forth more abundant harvest. Such a field the great Teacher of Galilee had found in the ministry of curative preaching. With the assurance gained from the understanding of his words and works, and with the background of public appearances extending over a period of years, Mary Baker Eddy was prepared to expand her area of preaching. Now appeared the first signs of a distinguished future clouded with storm. The power of the Bible, the Science of the coexistence of God and man, was to be expounded by its Discoverer from the orthodox pulpit.

Still in the modest home in Lynn, Mrs. Eddy sought of Spirit preparation to enable her to accept an invitation from the pastor of the Shawmut Avenue Baptist Church in Boston to occupy his pulpit. Of this experience in 1878 she writes:

The congregation so increased in number the pews were not sufficient to seat the audience and benches were used in the aisles. At the close of my engagement we parted in Christian fellowship, if not in full unity of doctrine.

Our last vestry meeting was made memorable by eloquent addresses from persons who feelingly testified to having been healed through my preaching. Among other diseases cured they specified cancers. The cases described had been treated and given over by physicians of the popular schools of medicine, but I had not heard of these cases till the persons who divulged their secret joy were healed. A prominent churchman agreeably informed the congregation that many others present had been healed under my preaching, but were too timid to testify in public. (Retrospection and Introspection, p. 15.)

Primitive Christianity was again touching the people as Mrs. Eddy poured forth her revelation of the Scriptures. Its nature and power were the same as they had been on the shores of Galilee.

After this Mrs. Eddy lectured in Parker Memorial Hall in Boston, where her first audiences were small. As the meetings continued, the congregations grew until the hall, seating some four hundred persons, was crowded. Standing before these assemblies Mrs. Eddy was an impressive figure. Slender, graceful, and erect, filled with the majesty of divine anointing, she seemed always to be imparting wisdom freshly drawn from wells of salvation. Looking beyond the finite to the infinite her countenance seemed alight with spiritual radiance. In her movements there was animation, but never agitation. There seemed to be in her consciousness a fountain of knowledge of Life ever springing forth in peaceful, persistent strength. One could not look at her without being aware of her holy calling. Speaking of her first glimpse of Mrs. Eddy, my mother, Mrs. Annie Rogers Michael, involuntarily uttered the words, "The moment I saw her I knew that I was in the presence of one inspired of God." As Mrs. Michael became a pupil of Mrs. Eddy's and saw her at intervals covering a period of thirty years, that impression lasted and deepened.

Eloquent voices were heard in the New England metropolis at this time. Edward Everett Hale occupied a Congregational pulpit with distinction, and Phillips Brooks was the eminent rector of Trinity Church. Mrs. Eddy valued his statement, "God has not given us vast learning to solve all the problems, or unfailing wisdom to direct all the wanderings of our brothers' lives; but He has given to every one of us the power to be spiritual, and by our spirituality to lift and enlarge and enlighten the lives we touch" (*Christian Science Sentinel,* January 6, 1906, p. 294). Her annotation to this statement reads, "The secret of my life is in the above."

Daring to discourse from the pulpit in company with such illustrious preachers; daring to present intransigent religious ideas and to support them with Christian healing, was no ordinary accomplishment.

Literature, philosophy, science, and art flourished in Boston in those postwar years, and attracted progressive thought. Some receptive students of the ideal and some who preferred to cling to their grandparents' concepts were curious if not eager to hear what the lady from Lynn had to say.

Unnumbered thousands who have now studied the Christian Science textbook in connection with the Bible know that Christian Science proclaims one infinite God, good, as Life, Truth, and Love, as Mind, thereby declaring the unreality of evil. They also know that Christian Science teaches man's absolute likeness to God, hence his entire spirituality, as stated in Genesis 1:27. Mrs. Eddy never departed from these basic premises in her preaching.

These truths taught by Christ Jesus needed to be rediscerned and reiterated in their primal purity. When the Master first stated that there is one universal cause and parent and one offspring, spiritual man in the likeness of Mind, the various sects and nationalities in Palestine were bewildered and amazed at his utterances. Never before had the gentle doctrine of one universal parentage blessed the lives of men and women, slave and free, conquered and conqueror, priest and penitent, soldier and civilian, ruler and masses. With this teaching the volatile beliefs of a humanized deity, of class distinctions, inequality of sexes, pagan idolatry, and barbarity began to evaporate.

The reappearing of the theology of Jesus in Christian Science has brought to this age the law of divine healing and has explained the metaphysics of Christ, Truth. The dispelling of evil in order that spiritual, harmonious living may abound, has always been the aim of the church. But the result of centuries of consecrated endeavor in this direction bespeaks something lacking in man-made creeds and doctrines.

The Nazarene defined evil as "a liar, and the father of it" (John 8:44), as that which claims to be fact, but in which there is no truth. Paul, in writing of overcoming evil, put it this way: "Awake thou that sleepest, and arise from the dead, and Christ shall give thee light" (Ephesians 5:14). Both Jesus and Paul spoke from the standpoint of instruction accompanied by demonstration.

In declaring the unreality of evil Mrs. Eddy followed this original Christian teaching. Like Jesus, she did not ignore evil appearing in the form of sin, sickness, mortality, error. She took case after case of suffering and, through her understanding of God's allness, healed each one. Thus she reduced phases of evil, disease, injuries, drunkenness, insanity to their native nothingness as did the Master.

Mrs. Eddy then sought to learn how mythical evil could even appear to exist. To do this she scientifically analyzed the terms "animal magnetism" and "mesmerism," which were in current use. It became clear to her that, even as the sleeper is mesmerized to believe that his dream is real, so is the daydream of material existence but a mesmeric state, ended only by the dreamer's waking to the spiritual fact that man is ever the offspring of God.

Mrs. Eddy used the terms "animal magnetism" and "mesmerism" to define this seeming action and acceptance of the mortal dream. In their last analysis these are names for the nonactivity of nothing and not appellations for mysterious power. This explanation of the falsity of mortal existence is in agreement with Paul's injunction to wake and rise from that which is already dead, nonexistent. This basic nullifying of evil reintroduced the prevention as well as the cure for mankind's woes.

These and other fundamental aspects of Christian faith not yet heard in other pulpits, Mrs. Eddy preached. Her favorite text was the First Commandment, "Thou shalt have no other gods before me" (Exodus 20:3). She wrote:

It demonstrates Christian Science. It inculcates the triunity of God, Spirit, Mind; it signifies that man shall have no other spirit or mind but God, eternal good, and that all men shall have one Mind. The divine Principle of the First Commandment bases the Science of being, by which man demonstrates health, holiness, and life eternal. One infinite God, good, unifies men and nations; constitutes the brotherhood of man; ends wars; fulfils the Scripture, "Love thy neighbor as thyself;" annihilates pagan and Christian idolatry,—whatever is wrong in social, civil, criminal, political, and religious codes; equalizes the sexes; annuls the curse on man, and leaves nothing that can sin, suffer, be punished or destroyed. (Science and Health, p. 340.)

Here was trenchant wisdom cutting through the surface of religious belief to the essence of God. Here was a sermon given without intent to please, but with desire to arouse and regenerate mankind. This preacher spoke not only to those gathered to hear her but to the human race for all time. She declared the Science of Life, the Science of Christ, without doubt or timidity. She felt the waves of criticism beating against this Rock, but the power of Love going out to mankind was stronger than the tide of hate flowing in, and turned it back.

Her discourses were varied. She amplified her text but never forsook its basic substance. Her bold originality sprang from her ability to interpret the Scriptures spiritually and confirm her statements with healing works. This put false theological teachings in the crucible of Truth. She presented Christian Science not only as the way to think, but also as the Science of living. With spiritual authority she expounded the laws of God and explained their adaptability to human need. Her exalted discernment was ever blessed with compassion for sin-sick humanity. She never mentally stooped to the distressing beliefs of those who came to her for help, but lifted them on wings of healing to feel the altitude of her vision. The truth which she declared, demanded and received her full allegiance.

The experience of preaching taught Mrs. Eddy that the orthodox pulpit resisted pure Christian Science. She saw that she could not win the church for the promulgation of her revelation unless she adulterated the message. But it was possible to develop a church of her own. This plan for organization first took shape in the home of Mrs. Margaret Dunshee in Charlestown, Massachusetts, in August, 1879. For some time services were held in parlors and in various other places until eventually The First Church of Christ, Scientist, was established in Hawthorne Hall at No. 2 Park Street, in Boston. Mrs. Eddy had been ordained pastor of the church by its officers and directors in accord with the Congregational method.

Progress demanded that Mrs. Eddy and her husband move to Boston, where they would be in closer touch with the expanding church organization. Some of the students were reluctant to have the close association between teacher and pupil, which was possible in Lynn, terminated by the forward trend. Others did not wish to be guided any longer by their teacher, and set out for themselves to teach and practice a pseudo-method of healing. One evening, a few months prior to leaving Lynn, Mr. and Mrs. Eddy attended a students' meeting. To their amazement a group presented a statement in which they accused her of being unworthy to carry on the Christian Science Cause. In this dark moment disloyalty menaced the accomplishment of years.

As teacher and healer with the lambs of her flock Mrs. Eddy had proved infinitely tender, patient, loving, and firm in the truth. Now, as organizer and Leader, she must protect the infant church committed to her care. After fruitless pleadings with the rebellious group not to allow evil motives to deceive them, she recognized their temporary inability to comprehend and obey the demands of Christian Science. Within a few days she removed them from her church and left the loyal members free to advance with her. Herein was shown a sign of leadership which was to endure through many vicissitudes until Christian Science churches should rise throughout the civilized world.

Before moving to Boston Mrs. Eddy completed her

revision of the third edition of Science and Health. Then she and Mr. Eddy went to Washington to examine the copyright laws. Her husband went so thoroughly into the matter that the copyrights of Mrs. Eddy's writings have been a bulwark for the spreading of unadulterated Christian Science. Missionaries were also sent out North, South, and West to acquaint other sections of the United States with the Christian Science textbook and to perform the cures promised therein. Slowly but surely the movement was taking form.

Mrs. Eddy was improving in her presentation of Christian Science through writing, teaching, and lecturing. Resisting any desire to shrink into obscurity and peace, she girded up the loins of her mind for a wider sphere of action. Looking beyond the borders of Lynn to the world, her revelation defined further steps in organization. As a stream gathering strength and depth rises to cover the rocks in its course, so the Christian Science movement left its narrow banks, sweeping beyond obstructions to wider shores.

XII

Spiritual Pioneering

HE eighties were full of import for the Christian Science movement. In these days Mrs. Eddy said in substance: "Christian Scientists are to the religious world, what backwoodsmen are to civilized America,—pioneers, who have much rough work to do" (*The Christian Science Journal,* May, 1887, p. 98). The hewing down of many obstacles, the plowing of furrows in new and wider fields, the uprooting of stubborn stumps of polytheism, superstition, religious prejudice, and imposition, all this must be done before general thought would be prepared for the planting of the seed of Truth. This could not be accomplished without personal sacrifice by the pioneers, without unwavering vision and courage. Then a harvest worth the reaping would reward their labor.

It required the pioneering strength of Paul for Mrs. Eddy, in 1882, to move to Boston, and in the Athens of the New World continue to preach a knowable God by whose Word the sick were healed. Whereas in Lynn scores had been healed and regenerated, in

Boston there would be hundreds and thousands to be helped. Hawthorne Hall, with its seating room of about two hundred, proved inadequate after a time. Then the larger Chickering Hall was procured and soon was filled to capacity.

The swift growth of Christian Science in these years was mainly due to the healing work carried on by the Leader and her followers. Disregardful of herself, Mrs. Eddy never used her religion for personal gain, but always for universal good; to help all men to know themselves as sons of God. No lesser motive than that of faithfully conveying her vision could survive in the burning light of her revelation of Truth. She cared not what others thought of her, so long as self-examination showed a steadfast, inner response to God's directing. She never loomed larger than her message nor failed to fulfill its demands. She came to bring the city a benediction which was to last beyond her lifetime.

There are those who regard the city as the gateway to fame and fortune; others, as the dispenser of favor hiding its flotsam under rainbow foam, as an arbiter weighing failure in the scales with success. Yet there is an unseen city of spiritual consciousness whose gates open toward glory for all. Mrs. Eddy and her husband went to Boston to spread news of this City of God, the City "which lieth foursquare," described with unmistakable clearness in more recently discovered sayings of Jesus:

> Let not him who seeks . . . cease until he finds, and when he finds he shall be astonished; astonished he shall reach the kingdom, and having reached the kingdom he shall rest. . . . and the kingdom of Heaven is within you; and whoever shall know himself shall find it. (Strive therefore?) to know yourselves, and ye shall be aware that ye are the sons of the (almighty?) Father; (and?) ye shall know that ye are in (the city of God?), and ye are (the city?). (New Sayings of Jesus, Oxford University Press.)

Soon after coming to Boston, in the home on Columbus Avenue where Mr. and Mrs. Eddy had settled, she faced a cruel blow. Mr. Eddy passed on. She met this great loss, not so much with human fortitude, as with unwavering conviction that God is the only and forever Life of man. This meant man's individuality indestructible in Spirit. She could not believe in both death and eternal Life. She must choose one or the other. She chose eternal Life.

The faithful companion who had eased the burdens of her he so earnestly loved had treated too lightly a discordant condition of his own. Asa Eddy's neglect of his personal welfare had its tragic result. His was possibly the first clear perception and appreciation of Mrs. Eddy as the Discoverer and Founder of Christian Science. His pioneer work in the practice of healing, the formation of a Sunday school, the teaching of the Metaphysical College, and the securing of copyrights on Mrs. Eddy's publications, have endeared his memory to all Christian Scientists.

The accumulating demands of the Church of Christ, Scientist, compelled Mrs. Eddy, as always before, to lean upon the nearness of divine Love for all her help. Because of this, the loss of her cherished companion was ameliorated. Her spiritual womanhood triumphed over the mortal. Again she set her face toward the future alone; that future which she knew rested in God's hands.

Further trouble concerning the movement demanded immediate attention. The previous disaffection of a student who had been entrusted with many of Mrs. Eddy's affairs in Lynn had taken a disturbing turn. He had published a pamphlet entitled "Christianity, or the Understanding of God as Applied to the Healing of the Sick," in which thirty pages of her writings had been used without stating their author. His endeavor was to disparage Mrs. Eddy and discredit her discovery. This plagiarism was referred to in no uncertain terms in Mr. Eddy's preface to the third edition of Science and Health which was released from the press about this time. In the light of the ironclad copyrights which he had secured in Washington, the

Federal Court forbade the recalcitrant student to publish any further pamphlets, and ordered the destruction of all existing ones.

From the year 1882 on, the Christian Science movement withstood all attacks against it and prospered. This dynamic doctrine caused New England to feel a definite tugging at its theological and therapeutical roots. Throughout the country there were evidences of the leaven of Truth at work. Arousing opposition or acceptance wherever its growth demanded acknowledgment in a world of progressive thought, Christian Science could no longer be ignored.

In one of Boston's suburban Protestant churches a number of its members withdrew because of the pastor's attack on Christian Science. Another minister was asked by his congregation to resign for a similar reason. In a church in New York State a clergyman left his pulpit after witnessing the healing of a case of hip disease abandoned as hopeless by a skillful surgeon. This clergyman stated that he had no right to continue to preach unless he could do the Christian healing work. Mrs. Eddy must have been greatly encouraged by these and other evidences of growing public enlightenment. Many instances of unquestionable cures wrought by others through spiritual means brought her added assurance and joy, for they confirmed anew the impartial nature of that power which had instantaneously healed her and led her on to the comprehension of divine Science.

One of these instances occurred as follows: a gentlewoman called at 571 Columbus Avenue and asked to see the Discoverer of Christian Science. She had come a long distance to speak with the woman whose teachings had saved her life. Mrs. Eddy granted her an interview and heard from her the story of her healing. A semi-invalid most of her life because of prolapsus, this woman had been sent home from a sanatorium with the medical verdict of having only six months to live. A friend suggested to her husband that he ask the help of a pupil of Mrs. Eddy's who happened to be stopping in the town. This suggestion was at first rejected because, as a devoted churchman, he felt that spiritual teaching and healing could come only through apostolic succession. When it was further explained to him that the healing was accomplished by understanding prayer and the same spirit through which the early Christians performed their cures, he gave his consent.

The only impression of the meeting with the Christian Scientist which remained with the invalid was one of indignation because she had been asked if she believed in one omnipotent God. Replying with some heat, she had averred that she was a good churchwoman and said every Sunday in the creed, "I believe in God the Father Almighty, Maker of heaven and earth."

As she lay on her bed that night, these familiar words from the creed kept repeating themselves in her consciousness. There was a full moon shining through her window. As she watched it she thought, "God has held up the moon for centuries without muscles, bones, or sinews." Then she asked herself, "By what means has God held it there?" And the answer came, "By divine laws." Then she reasoned, "If there is one God of heaven and earth, He has made those same laws to hold up every part of my being."

When the morning came, packings that had been used to support fallen organs were removed and the invalid said to her nurse: "I will not hold you responsible for anything that may happen, but today God is going to be God to me, or nothing." In the late afternoon suddenly the suffering ceased, and she knew that God had healed her. Years of devotion to the words of a creed had done nothing to help her, but one clear glimpse of the divine truth of their statement permanently set her free.

When the story was finished Mrs. Eddy said, "Why, dear, you were healed straight from God, just the way I was." Healing such as this lifted Christian Science pathology beyond the assertions that it was helpful only for nervous troubles; that it was the effect of one human mind upon another; or that the beneficiaries would have, in due course, recovered their health.

However, false statements about this new-old religion kept appearing in newspapers and pamphlets, in lectures and sermons. Mockery and rivalry met every achievement. Anonymous letters were sent to Mrs. Eddy containing threats to blow up the hall where services were held. The congregation by this time had increased to some six hundred persons. The general public still thought religious healing to be a pious fraud, and Christian Science teachings were regarded as mere optimism. The insistence of these teachings that strict morality was essential to spiritual progress and divine healing, roused some opposition. Taking account of these storm signals, Mrs. Eddy prayed to be shown how to steer her course. The answer to her prayer came in the wise resolve to start the first Christian Science periodical, which she named *Journal of Christian Science.*

To the Leader's activities which included revision of Science and Health from time to time to clarify its meaning, preaching, teaching, healing, and in every way assisting her students, was now added the detailed task of being the publisher of the *Journal* which was launched in 1883. In its columns she answered attacks upon her movement, instructed her growing flock in their conduct as workers, and safeguarded the teachings of Christian Science from corruption.

Most of Mrs. Eddy's contributions to these early numbers of the *Journal* are now included in her invaluable book entitled "Miscellaneous Writings." They show, among other characteristics of the author, deep spiritual understanding of the Bible, keen detection of error as always impersonal, and delightful humor. She was as patient with her public as with her pupils, resilient under onslaught, and expert in wielding the pen of the Spirit. She emerged from every encounter as the victor who had stripped her opponent of his venom and covered his defeat with loving-kindness.

The Columbus Avenue home was a teeming center of enterprise. Because of ever-growing demands upon her time the Leader was forced to reconstruct her household. Mr. Eddy's loving foresight during the latter part of his lifetime had led him to search for someone who could serve his wife in a confidential capacity. With this thought in mind he had journeyed to Lawrence, Massachusetts, to inquire about a Mr. Calvin A. Frye who lived there. Favorably impressed by what he had been told, he counseled Mrs. Eddy to avail herself of the services of this student. Mr. Frye had studied with her in Lynn about a year before and from then on had continued in the healing practice. Mrs. Eddy knew only too well that anyone so closely connected with her important work, as he would be, would require, among other qualities, faithfulness, discretion, and obedience. After careful examination of his thought and general fitness, Mrs. Eddy engaged Mr. Frye to assist her. He kept her books, acted as her purchasing agent, relieved her of a considerable amount of correspondence, and also appeared for her at different gatherings. His service, dictated by devotion as well as duty, began two months after her husband passed on and continued to the end of her earthly sojourn.

The Christian Science movement was passing through a transitional stage. The demands upon Mrs. Eddy's time and willingness far exceeded the ability of one individual. Publicity of the healings accomplished through herself and her students aroused both interest and opposition. The methods of releasing the teachings to the public were still inadequate. Revelation was a matter between herself and God; organization involved hundreds of her followers. Early steps of systematization were immature, but ever tended toward the complete form later presented in the Manual of The Mother Church.

Visible signs of the progress of the Christian Science movement were unmistakable. Besides the ever-swelling congregation in Boston, there were groups throughout the land composed of those who had been healed and drawn together by a burning desire to understand the new light thrown on the Bible. There was a growing demand for Mrs. Eddy's writings from a host of students resolved to devote their lives to Christian Science work. It was noticeable that when Mrs. Eddy's teachings touched other lives, they not only delivered men from discord but awakened within them the zeal to serve.

The eighties were drawing to a close. Mary Baker Eddy had pursued her way of discovery and establishment of scientific religion for more than twenty years. The period of aloneness with her vision was past. Many were climbing the mount of transfiguration and, inspired by her instructions, were spreading the message of Christian healing.

XIII

The Movement Unfolds

HE nineteenth century was notable for the achievement of women in national affairs. This was particularly apparent in New England. A surge of reform was breaking against the bastions of tradition. Breastworks of slavery were weakened by the earnest eloquence of Harriet Beecher Stowe in her "Uncle Tom's Cabin." Barriers of unequal suffrage were breached by Lucy Stone. The persistent courage of Jane Addams helped to destroy the general apathy towards the evils of city slums. In the medical field openings for women were won through the intrepid achievements of Elizabeth Blackwell. Other distinguished names, such as Julia Ward Howe, Elizabeth Cady Stanton, Clara Barton, and Susan B. Anthony, compel the admission that women played their part, and no uncertain one, in the moral pioneering of these years.

In the instance of each of these noble women reform was directed against a specific type of wrong. But the full force of the surge of Spirit swept through Mary Baker Eddy against the entire claim of evil. Where other methods of reform sought to deal with "the tree of knowledge of good and evil" by breaking off its branches, Christian Science pulled up the roots.

The twentieth century was to experience calamity in hitherto undreamed-of phases. Hatred, cruelty, and destruction would sweep over a great part of the civilized world as human inventions were turned against mankind. Materiality was to fail at the time of humanity's greatest dependence upon it. There would be need for deeper analysis of events, their mental cause and trend, and for divine wisdom in dealing with the problems they presented. Terms such as magnetism, mesmerism, and aggressive suggestion used by Mrs. Eddy, which at the time had sounded strange, would be found in press reports of world news. The man in the street was to learn that evil influences can seem to operate only so long as they are accepted as power. Once they are seen to be unreal and are forsaken because they are untrue, they begin to vanish in the light of understanding.

It was imperative that these deceptions should be foreseen and foretold before such an era came; that men should be forewarned of evil's fabulousness, and forearmed to overcome it through comprehension of supreme good. Mrs. Eddy had already written in her textbook the following significant statements:

> This material world is even now becoming the arena for conflicting forces. On one side there will be discord and dismay; on the other side there will be Science and peace. The breaking up of material beliefs may seem to be famine and pestilence, want and woe, sin, sickness, and death, which assume new phases until their nothingness appears. These disturbances will continue until the end of error, when all discord will be swallowed up in spiritual Truth. (Science and Health, p. 96.)

Such exposure of evil's native nothingness comes only from the pure source which brought to St. John, on the Isle of Patmos, the vision of the new heaven and earth. Spiritual vision comes when divine Mind writes its thoughts in the hearts of men, and this heart was prepared for such inscription. Whereas others spoke and wrote uncertainly of unseen reality, Mary Baker Eddy declared and demonstrated with scientific exactness the things of Spirit. The quiet dignity of utter sincerity was hers. Stopping at no attainment, she moved forward in endless accomplishment as the spiritual Science which she announced transformed the world of thought.

In the simply furnished house with its gray stone front in Boston, where Christian Science was now being sought, great events were transpiring. A woman declaring the eternal spirituality of the universe and man was daring to live in increasing measure what she declared, and was teaching others to do likewise.

Mrs. Eddy was carrying on all the work of the Metaphysical College. Gradually she gained confidence and experience in articulating and substantiating her message. Those who attended her College classes felt the humility, strength, and inner glory which permeated all her teaching. Honesty and spiritual power characterized her every word. That this teaching might be fruitful she wrote to some of her pupils taking the class work: "Think *alone* in your rooms of all that I have said, and let the seed take *root* before stirring it" (Mrs. Eddy's letter to Normal class in 1887).

As yet the promotion and expansion of the Christian Science movement seemed to depend almost entirely upon Mrs. Eddy's personal direction. Her teaching occupied much of her time. In 1884 a Normal class was held. The ten members of this class were the first ones authorized to give instruction in Christian Science. After the College had flourished for nearly nine years and had sent out many students, including teachers, in spite of the hundreds who were clamoring for admission, Mrs. Eddy closed the doors in order "that the spirit of Christ might have freer course among its students and all who come into the understanding of Divine Science" (*The Christian Science Journal,* February, 1890, p. 566).

The Christian Scientist Association which Mrs.

Eddy had formed in the middle seventies at no time included all of her pupils. In accord with her instruction, those pupils who had been made teachers in 1884 commenced to form Associations of their pupils in 1886; also in the same year a National Christian Scientist Association was organized, which included members from at least fifteen states and from Canada.

The heart and soul of the Christian Science movement was not, and never would be, in mere grouping of numbers, but rather in the pentecostal vision of the Founder of the movement and of her true followers. While Mrs. Eddy walked all the way of human procedure, she unswervingly held her gaze to divine causation; she listened for the voice of Truth to say, "This is the way," and then moved on in utter obedience. The divine afflatus unfolded the early progress of Christian Scientists and maintains this progress.

The light of a widening horizon kept every detail of the movement within the focus of the Leader's thought and accentuated it. The original title of the textbook had been "Science and Health." This was changed to "Science and Health with Key to the Scriptures." This book reached its fiftieth edition in 1891—an outstanding achievement for any author. Mrs. Eddy augmented her literary productions during the latter half of the eighties. One pamphlet, "Historical

Sketch of Metaphysical Healing," later became part of her book "Retrospection and Introspection," and another pamphlet entitled "Rudiments and Rules of Divine Science" developed into the book "Rudimental Divine Science." "Christian Science: No and Yes" and "Unity of Good and Unreality of Evil" appeared and were revised to bear the titles, respectively, of "No and Yes" and "Unity of Good."

Extra moments were crowded with voluminous correspondence. Then *The Christian Science Journal* required more and more attention. It passed through various literary vicissitudes until it reached a flourishing condition six years after its inception, when Mrs. Eddy presented this periodical and its financial profits to the National Christian Scientist Association. In 1898 it became the property of The Christian Science Publishing Society. In this periodical, aside from various articles and testimonies of healing, appeared advertisements of teachers and practitioners in many states. Through its columns Mrs. Eddy spoke to Christian Scientists throughout New England, in the Central States, on the shores of the Pacific and in Canada. The widespread reappearing of Christian healing was fast becoming the most momentous tidings to reach humanity in sixteen centuries.

Mrs. Eddy was still preaching on Sundays and lecturing once a week in her parlors. She also allowed some of her pupils who lived at the College to receive their patients there. Through her doorway from dawn to dusk passed groups of earnest workers, newcomers impelled by curiosity, and those seeking healing and teaching. This diligent woman was accessible to them all, gracious, unhurried, and considerate, the shining energy of her mission permeating all her contacts. She was as buoyantly eager to disseminate her message as she was to receive it. There was little opportunity for seclusion, and yet there was need for gathering fresh wisdom from the divine source with which to coordinate and direct the expansion of her work.

From the first Mrs. Eddy was aware of the infinite scope of her discovery and its specific adaptability with respect to every human need. This would account for her patient persistence in founding an organization which would function both locally and universally. While establishing the Christian Science church in Boston she knew its mission to be world-wide. Deeply concerned in the welfare of each member, she was already visualizing congregations undreamed of by those about her. To her, the infinitesimal opportunity was always a part of the infinite possibility.

By this time there were people in inaccessible places who had been healed of serious difficulties by reading

Science and Health. Active students and the church publication, the *Journal,* had awakened interest in Christian Science in widespread communities and cities. Students in the Middle West, as well as those in the East, were performing cures which though divinely natural to those who had accepted the power of God with men seemed miraculous to the general public. Not only the freeing of slaves achieved by the Civil War, but the release of hopeless invalids and victims of sin through practice of scientific religion, gave promise of a new era of liberty throughout the land.

During the year in which Mrs. Eddy taught her first Normal class in Boston there had come a request from Chicago for a class to be taught in that city. Mrs. Eddy tried to find a student able to meet this need but did not succeed. It seemed impossible for her to leave her important duties in Boston, but finally there came the clear decision to go herself, and remain in Chicago a month. One of her students and Mr. Frye, who made all the arrangements, accompanied her. This proved a wise move, for from the nucleus of a class taught on the West Side gradually sprang the growth of Christian Science in that great city and on to the western borders of the United States. In a few months an institute for teaching was opened in Chicago and another in California.

This journey away from the local borders of her work gave the Leader a new perspective. The movement had passed beyond the range of personal supervision; yet she alone was capable of directing its onward course. There were teachers whose work she could not carefully watch. There were practitioners whose methods she could not test. The fluid form of her Church and Association, which, with her College, comprised her organization, was not cohesive enough to hold together the expanding parts, nor was it elastic enough to provide for prodigious growth.

The situation called for a central form of government which would be directly related to the remotest functioning of the Cause. It was well that Mrs. Eddy knew how to lean upon a higher wisdom than her own, otherwise this stupendous task could not have been carried through. She sought for a permanent form of government, which, while guiding human action, would not limit individual growth. She knew that at the apex of the movement must stand the Christ, the true idea of God, dispelling false beliefs and revealing the way of salvation. While there must be church laws of organization, the movement must remain under divine control.

Gradually the next decade was to give form to this concept.

XIV

Foundation Laid

T this critical time in the establishment of Christian Science, threatened idolatry of the Leader's personality would have endangered the course of the movement. But Mrs. Eddy's farseeing nature directed the stream of her followers' gratitude and affection back to its fount, the infinite motherhood of Love, God.

Part of Mrs. Eddy's great revelation was the discernment of the motherhood as well as the fatherhood of God. Herein appeared the nourishing, satisfying, complete nature of Deity, of the Life that is always Mother Love, omnipotent Love, ever-present, changeless Love.

Those who felt the touch of divine Mother Love expressed in their Leader's every word and action did not always discern Love's impersonal nature. The appellation of "mother" was given to her by students and, while she permitted it for a season, the continued use of the term was against her wishes and finally contrary to her orders. This, Mrs. Eddy patiently helped her adherents to understand.

Doubtless it was difficult for those who had little conception of Mrs. Eddy's unparalleled spiritual vision, and of the majesty of divine disclosures, to understand her reasons for forthcoming actions. To those less absorbed than she in the world's spiritual progress, these actions seemed at times dictatorial, nonessential, even irritating. There were moments when she felt keenly the misunderstanding of her purpose by those most closely associated with her. Her joy came not so much from human relationships as from her conscious oneness with God. Not what others did for her, but what she did for them enriched her life. Her story is one of magnificent triumph over adverse events and deliberate aggressions. Better than anyone, she knew the nature of the supreme power which impelled and upheld her through the years.

To be released from the overlapping duties and demands at the Columbus Avenue residence where she taught her classes, Mrs. Eddy in 1887 bought a house at 385 Commonwealth Avenue.

Here she once more picked up the threads of her son's life—that son whose privilege it was to love and cherish one of the greatest figures of history, but who, unseeing, turned the other way. She had not seen him for nearly ten years when word came that he and his family were arriving from the West to pay her a visit.

At this time George Glover was about forty-three years of age, a rough plainsman interested in prospecting for gold and silver mines. He knew nothing of the finer side of life and was totally uncomprehensive of his mother's lofty nature and endeavor. Her home being the center of many exacting demands, she rented a house for George and his family and did much to help them socially and financially. But the gulf between these two was not to be bridged. He could not understand her teachings nor fit into her way of living. She was compelled to relinquish any hope of intimate companionship with him. But this did not deter her from giving her son and his family pecuniary assistance when they returned to their home, and also in later years. During this visit the only baptismal service ever held in the Christian Science church took place. Mrs. Eddy christened twenty-nine children, among whom were her three grandchildren.

Not long after this experience with George Glover, Mrs. Eddy, feeling the need of someone close to her to assist in her affairs, sought among her students one whom she could take into her family circle. She chose Dr. E. J. Foster, and legally adopted him as a son. He was about the age of her own son and was a graduate of Hahnemann Medical College in Philadelphia, holding diplomas from homeopathic and regular schools of medicine. He had been attracted to Christian Science through the healing of a friend and later studied in the Metaphysical College with Mrs. Eddy.

Dr. Foster-Eddy was appreciative of his teacher's motherly attitude toward him and for a while was a help to her. He taught one class in the College, took care of much of the publishing business, and was a comfort to her in their home life. Though nearing her sixty-seventh year her cares were increasing. She was desirous of training her students to assume responsibilities, and to look not to her, but to God, for wisdom in conducting the affairs of the Christian Science movement.

Mrs. Eddy's adopted son stayed with her over a period of about eight years and then went his way. He finally proved unworthy to carry out her wishes, unreliable in judgment, and more inclined to seek popularity than spirituality. With the same kindness with which she had welcomed him into her home life, she let him go. She always spoke of him graciously and later made financial provision for him.

While Mrs. Eddy was adjusting her home circle, the clamoring demands of outside affairs increased. The National Christian Scientist Association held its third annual meeting in Chicago in June of the year 1888. Delegates were invited to attend from many states. Mrs. Eddy realized that this gathering would afford opportunity to observe the collective action of her students and help her in determining the form of government best adapted to the growing movement. She therefore decided to go to Chicago as an observer only. Through the *Journal* she sent word to the Field to let nothing prevent her pupils from attending the convention, which she regarded as of vital importance.

As teacher and Leader, Mrs. Eddy's labor was incessant. There was no time for mere enjoyment of her fruitage. There was always something more to be done. She could not know the great depths of love and reverence which lay in the hearts of those who had never seen her, but who had been raised from beds of pain and liberated from bondage of every sort by the Science which she had revealed to the world. Her every word came to them as the utterance of a seer. Their obedience to her guidance in spiritual welfare was spontaneous. The grain of gratitude was a ripened harvest awaiting the reaping.

On the second day of the gathering an open meeting for visiting Christian Scientists was held at Central Music Hall, where the number of eight hundred delegates was swelled by the public to an attendance of about four thousand. The newspapers had advertised Mrs. Eddy's presence and, unknown to her, had stated that she would give the address of that day. She was utterly unaware of what was expected of her until her escort informed her just as she was about to take her seat upon the stage. There was a moment of hesitation, a gesture as of protest, an upward looking as though to see, beyond the crowd, a greater Presence. Then the audience rose spontaneously and stood in silent tribute before that slender figure advancing to the front of the platform.

Into the silence the words of the first verse of the ninety-first Psalm rang in clear tones, reaching to the farthest corner of the auditorium: "He that dwelleth in the secret place of the most High shall abide under the shadow of the Almighty." Without hesitancy or apparent effort, without a single preparatory note, this text was unfolded into a discourse which held her audience enthralled. It was as though "the glory of the Lord shone round about them." It was this sense of God with her that touched the deepest feelings of men and women, held the pencils of the reporters still, and left an inerasable memory with her listeners.

When she ceased speaking the audience broke like a wave against the platform. As the multitude thronged her, love and joy burst all bounds and flowed in a flood tide of gratitude. Eager hands reached out to touch her. Some strove to tell her of healings which her book had brought them. Others sought healing. Eleven cases of deliverance from disease were recorded that day. Still others, looking for the first time upon the face of her whose discovery had opened for them undreamed-of depths of spiritual vision, knew that she had received from the supreme intelligence that which she had shared with them. There was so much of the divine about her that he who touched the hem of her thought waked in some measure to his own oneness with the Father.

With difficulty a way was cleared to the carriage waiting to take Mrs. Eddy to her hotel. That evening found the drawing room, which had been hurriedly decorated for an informal reception, crowded with people awaiting her appearance. Finally she came, desirous of graciously receiving as many as she could. But the pressure of the crowd became so great that she withdrew, remarking that such methods did not further the Cause of Christian Science.

She was thinking of the furtherance of the Cause, not personal adulation. She had gone to Chicago to be better prepared to formulate a permanent church government. From this experience she saw that personality and popularity could be more perilous to a righteous cause than persecution. She was aware that the cries of adoration could turn to whispers of treachery. It was becoming more and more apparent to her that the structure of the Church must rest only upon divine Principle. There it could withstand the dangerous fluctuations of human thought and endure.

The incomplete account of Mrs. Eddy's Chicago address, entitled "Science and the Senses," published in "Miscellaneous Writings," contains among others this great statement: "Christian Science is an everlasting victor, and vanquishment is unknown to the omnipresent Truth. I must ever follow this line of light and battle" (p. 105).

When the Christian Science Leader returned to Boston there was great need for the vision and courage implied in this utterance. Whispering treachery had been busy in the ranks of students in the East while praise had soared in the Middle West. A group of thirty-six dissenters had taken steps to separate themselves from Mrs. Eddy's followers, but were determined that they should be merely dismissed, not expelled, as had been a former group in Lynn. They did not want to bear any stigma, but desired to be freed from their Leader's guidance though still using her teachings. They resorted to trickery to carry out their purpose, and persisted in this course for a year. During this time they even considered attempting to remove Mrs. Eddy from her position as Leader.

There were other disaffections. One student who had been most closely associated with the Leader withdrew. Another, who had attended the Chicago class, had become an exponent of "mental science" in the West. Two other students had strayed from the straight teaching and living of Christian Science. Time and again, those who departed from Mrs. Eddy's instructions built their frail attempts at leadership upon her words, adulterated their meanings, and lapsed into the oblivion of hypocrisy. At this time Mrs. Eddy wrote to one of her loyal pupils: "Our Father is steering in this red sea and will divide the waters and take the true Christian Scientists through on dry land and swallow up the troops of error" (Mrs. Eddy's letter to Annie Rogers Michael).

Mrs. Eddy had to defend her work not only from these internal assaults, but also from external aggression. Two of Mr. Quimby's followers, both active in propagating spurious "mental science," were in Boston. Their publications contained statements which sought to corrupt her teachings and deprive Mrs. Eddy of her rights as Discoverer and Leader of Christian Science. Just when she needed uninterrupted opportunity for prayer whereby to lay the mental cornerstone of the future structure of her movement, she had to deal with conditions that would weaken from within and assail from without. Attempts to impede the Cause and dishearten its Leader seemed endless.

This crucial period in the history of Christian Science needs to be evaluated to understand the character of its Founder. Mary Baker Eddy stood at the crossroads where both personal power and divine guidance beckoned. A world unaware awaited her choice of the road, for that choice, if right, meant great spiritual awakening for the human race. From "the pinnacle of praise" (Manual, p. 47) she had seen the kingdoms of the world. If she would take them, they were hers. She could wear the robes of rulership and be crowned with adoration. She could live in the luxury of popularity and command the obedience of multitudes. Aggrandizement and glorification were within her reach, if only she would take her hand out of God's.

Personal power beckoned in vain. Her thought never swerved from divine guidance. Neither lifted up by acclaim nor cast down by hostility, she kept steadfastly on her way.

Carefully scrutinizing the framework of her movement, wherever she found it resting upon personality she removed the underpinning and left only the parts based upon Principle. As has been previously mentioned, she closed the flourishing Metaphysical College in 1889. The Primary teaching was left to qualified students throughout the Field. She dissolved the Christian Scientist Association at the same time. With the unanimous consent of the members she also dissolved the Church. Several months previously she had resigned as pastor. However the Church continued to function informally until 1892, when it was re-formed.

The painstaking work of a quarter of a century seemed to be hanging in the balance. At the height of prosperity, never doubting the issue, she left her accomplishment in the hand of God who had initiated and prospered it. Her response to the supreme test of her character had not found her wanting. She knew that it was expedient for her followers that she go away, that Truth alone might direct them.

Of these eventful steps Mrs. Eddy wrote in the *Christian Science Journal* of February, 1890: "The dissolution of the visible organization of the Church is the sequence and complement of that of the College Corporation and Association. . . . The bonds of organization of the Church were thrown away, so that its members might assemble themselves together and 'provoke one another to good works' in the bond only of Love."

She later wrote in a letter to a student: "You recall his (Jesus) . . . turning water into wine for the marriage feast, and even being baptized to meet the necessity of 'suffer it to be so now for thus it becometh us to fulfil all righteousness.' His age or the age in which he lived required what he did and his wisdom caused his concession to its requirements in some instances. Just as this age requires organization to maintain Christian Science." (Mary Baker Eddy: A Life Size Portrait, by Dr. Lyman P. Powell, p. 311.)

XV

Church Concept

NOW appeared a definite course of action whereby Christian Scientists throughout the world could unite in organization while progressing in their understanding of absolute divine Science. The Mother Church, the visible form of Mrs. Eddy's inspired concept, organized in 1892, was the outcome of the Church of Christ, Scientist, founded in 1879 and dissolved in 1889. Earlier methods of procedure gave place to a permanent form of government. Previous congregational polity was superseded by a duly constituted Christian Science Board of Directors and a part of the membership known as First Members. The functions of the First Members were later delegated to the Board of Directors. The executive administration of the Church affairs, always under Mrs. Eddy's leadership, developed over a period of years until it became stabilized. This government reached its final form as now set forth in the Manual of The Mother Church.

This Manual provides the Rules and By-Laws essential for the central government of the Christian

Science movement. These rules direct the functioning of The Mother Church and arrange for self-government of all branch churches so that fundamental unity of action may be achieved. The duties of Christian Science teachers, practitioners, and workers throughout the Field are guided by these rules. The obedience of each church member to Christian Science is found in individual compliance with these By-Laws, and thereby with the Founder's vision of orderly unfoldment and limitless, cohesive expansion. Of them she wrote in 1895:

> The Rules and By-laws in the Manual of The First Church of Christ, Scientist, Boston, originated not in solemn conclave as in ancient Sanhedrim. They were not arbitrary opinions nor dictatorial demands, such as one person might impose on another. They were impelled by a power not one's own, were written at different dates, and as the occasion required. They sprang from necessity, the logic of events,—from the immediate demand for them as a help that must be supplied to maintain the dignity and defense of our Cause; hence their simple, scientific basis, and detail so requisite to demonstrate genuine Christian Science, and which will do for the race what absolute doctrines destined for future generations might not accomplish. (Miscellaneous Writings, p. 148.)

A paragraph in the Church Manual presents the foundation of the Christian Science Church in these few words: "THE FIRST CHURCH OF CHRIST, SCIENTIST, IN BOSTON, MASS., is designed to be built on the

Rock, Christ; even the understanding and demonstration of divine Truth, Life, and Love, healing and saving the world from sin and death; thus to reflect in some degree the Church Universal and Triumphant" (p. 19). This was the foundation laid by Christ Jesus. Because of this Mrs. Eddy was not merely optimistic, but certain, as to the means through which the revelation of Christian Science was to be disseminated and protected.

The early Christian Scientists, though understanding only an infinitesimal part of the plan which divine intelligence was unfolding to their Leader, were convinced of Mrs. Eddy's inspired guidance in all that pertained to Christian Science. They felt a zeal to do all that was asked of them, to be obedient to the Church rules for conduct, to press forward in the gain of spiritual perception, to heal continuously. Without this spirit among the workers the church structure would have been a hollow shell.

So long as the thoughts of Christian Scientists are fed from the same source whence came the revelation to the Founder of the denomination, they will see the reasons for this simple yet superb organization which functions to protect and support the spread of Christian Science. In this way only can "the Church Universal and Triumphant" appear.

Mrs. Eddy's withdrawal in person from the outward activities of the Christian Science movement, about a year after her return from Chicago, acted as an impetus in preserving her leadership. This step embodied her conviction that only through constant, radical reliance upon the one Mind could she conceive and establish a permanent instrumentality for demonstrating the revelation of Christian Science.

The need for her activity as the Founder of the movement was now demanding increasing thought and time. In order that she might accomplish this work, it was essential that she should be loosed from further participation in the general affairs of her followers. To effect this release she published a notice in the *Journal* in the form of seven rules, unequivocally stating that she was not to be consulted in routine Church or Association matters, or as to the contents of the *Journal*. She was to be excused from all consultations concerning family affairs, disaffections, and the conduct of members of the organization. Neither was she to be approached in connection with illness or treatment. It was imperative that she be freed to move in a wider area of thought and action. This was indicated by these final words of her communication: " . . . but I shall love all mankind—and work for their welfare" (*Christian Science Journal,* September, 1890, p. 249).

The founding of the Church included the choosing of students to fill responsible positions. This required discernment of character as well as just appraisal of fitness. Morality, honesty, fidelity, and consecration, as well as spiritual understanding, were essential in the church workers. There were pupils from farms in the White Mountains, rugged folk of stern, religious thought and dogged nature. There were intellectual persons from Boston and its vicinity. Among her followers were eager neophytes, impulsive Peters, and loving Johns. She must choose from among them those who loved Christian Science more than themselves.

Before seeking the retirement which the new phase of her work demanded, the Leader was to journey once more afield. She went to New York to speak to an audience of over one thousand people in Steinway Hall. She stood before them as one whose greatness lay in unseen spiritual victories and yet as one who had achieved amazing human success. As a preacher, she commanded large audiences, for her sermons were effectual in healing. As an author her original and arresting writings were much in demand both at home and abroad. Her following had expanded beyond the reaches of a single continent and her resources, now ample and continually mounting, were used for the promotion of her work, not for ease. Her human achievements announced the triumph of her spiritual knowing.

With the same modesty and strength which had characterized her appearance in Chicago, Mrs. Eddy spoke to her listeners in New York City. After her address she returned to the stage for over an hour to greet those desiring to speak with her. If there were some who marveled at her poise and power, they might have recalled the visit to New York, in 1850, of another famous woman, Jenny Lind. It is reported that after one of her great performances she was asked how she, just a slip of a woman, could stand before a vast audience with utter lack of self-consciousness and sing so compellingly. She replied, "I never have but one in my audience. I sing straight back to God, who gave me my voice."

Having withdrawn from various activities now delegated to others, there were to be three years of comparative aloofness from the encroaching selfishness of the human mind, the years between 1889 and 1892. Leaving the home on Commonwealth Avenue, Mrs. Eddy sought refuge first in Concord, New Hampshire, and then for a brief time in Roslindale, Massachusetts. Returning to Concord she finally took up her residence on a farm of about seventy acres just outside the city limits. The farmhouse on this property, which she purchased, was soon remodeled into a modest home suitable for quiet living and earnest praying.

Looking across the sloping meadows, Mrs. Eddy saw Bow, her birthplace, only a few miles away. She had climbed the hills of aspiration since the years spent at Bow. Illness, frailty, poverty, sorrow, scorn, and loneliness had all been vanquished. Yet Pleasant View, as her new estate was called, was not to be a resting place in her journey of life. The future was crowding the present with oncoming events. Far from deserting her mission, she was foreseeing its path of progress.

Up to the time Mrs. Eddy removed to Concord her experiences in developing a church were not satisfactory. No definite form of service had been consistently followed. In some instances the poison of "who shall be greatest?" tainted growing strength and schisms rose. The influx of adherents to the Cause had far outrun preparation for their coming. Undoubtedly Mrs. Eddy realized that the only solution for this situation was more divine directing and less human management. So she stayed with the source of her revelation to discern further its natural power of outward expression. She must be attentive to the divine utterance, oblivious of the human tumult. If the spire of Spirit was to rise above fluctuating human opinions, its builder and maker must be God.

Shortly after she moved to Pleasant View the idea of the Church of Christ, Scientist, became clarified in Mrs. Eddy's consciousness and objectified as The Mother Church in Boston, with branch churches throughout the United States and abroad. With deepening serenity of conviction Mary Baker Eddy was learning that a God-given idea is God-directed and God-protected. Not world-wide travel, but unfettered thinking, was unfolding her concept of a universal church. It was as though her spiritual vigor removed mountains, eliminated space, and brought the world to the threshold of the infinite.

The religious structure which gradually took shape in Mrs. Eddy's thought was not one of creed but of Truth and Love. It was not conceived to play upon the fears of men, to foster superstition, or to mold opinion. It appeared to fulfill the hopes of heaven, "to commemorate the word and works of our Master, which should reinstate primitive Christianity and its lost element of healing" (Manual, p. 17).

The great creeds of Christendom show the efforts of awakening Christian consciousness to realize and express progressive spiritual understanding. But the simple faith outlined in their early forms became lost through the centuries, and was finally replaced with critical opinions. It was both desirable and inevitable that the purity of Christianity, strengthened by understanding and proof, should again appear among men. In 1892, The First Church of Christ, Scientist, in Boston, adopted its Tenets, which require of the Church members comprehension of a knowable God made manifest in lives redeemed from sickness and sin. They commit the Christian Science worshiper to a life of demonstrated spiritual progress. It is no wonder that this religion has outlived the scoffing of the nineteenth century, and won the respect of the twentieth.

The Christian Science concept of religious structure, discerned by Mrs. Eddy was, as it were, the Christian Church "parting with its materiality" (Message for 1902, p. 5), rousing from slumber of speculation, breaking fetters of human hypotheses, shaking off lethargy, becoming aware of strength. It was as though the Church had at last stripped off outworn vestments of profession and put on beautiful garments of healing. No longer emasculated by sectarian beliefs, but vitalized by divine Truth, it was ready to reign on earth.

No need of sanctimonious pretense or subterfuge of spectacle was here. The Church felt and exercised its mastery over sin, disease, and death. It had the splendor of the wisdom of God to spread abroad. No longer with whispering lips must it breathe a message of hope, but with thundering voice it announced the presence of holiness among men. It was as though all the windows of the Church were thrown wide open, so that the clear shining of the Christ-light, uncolored and undimmed by mysticism and ignorance, might pierce the shadows and illumine the altars. The doors swung wide to every man, and the cup of spiritual communion was placed in every hand.

In that quiet home in Concord, Mary Baker Eddy visualized the future of the Christian Science movement, saw the dangers awaiting it, and felt God's hand sustaining and directing it. She foresaw it engirdling the globe, not primarily with numbers of temples, but with regenerated lives quickened to divine service in thoughts and deeds. She measured the growth not so much by assemblages as by the diminishing of sin and suffering wherever Christian Science was welcomed in. She looked into the hearts of her followers and saw "the living, palpitating presence of Christ, Truth" (Science and Health, p. 351), quickening and preserving their loyalty to divine Principle. And she predicted that "if the lives of Christian Scientists attest their fidelity to Truth . . . in the twentieth century every Christian church in our land, and a few in far-off lands, will approximate the understanding of Christian Science sufficiently to heal the sick in his name" (Pulpit and Press, p. 22).

Mrs. Eddy's part in this accomplishment was now outlined in bold relief. There was no possibility of withdrawal from demands which every day grew greater. Yet, the years were now threescore and ten and never had there been a period of leisure since that day in 1866 when her release from suffering had come.

About three centuries before this time, when undertaking the circumnavigation of the globe, the intrepid Drake prayed: "O Lord, when thou givest to thy servants to endeavor any great matter, grant us also to know that it is not the beginning, but the continuing of the same, until it be thoroughly finished, which yieldeth the true glory."

This valiant woman's labors were to continue until her revelation of Truth had encompassed the earth.

XVI

Church Edifice

T Pleasant View, Mrs. Eddy was a step removed from the world. A low fence marked the boundary of her acres, but did not define a limit of her graciousness. Far from shutting out events, her seclusion was shaping them. If people along her road wondered if she would "neighbor well" they soon found out. The milkman, coming to her door, felt her concern and help about obtaining water for his cattle. In a real estate transaction with an oversharp salesman she taught him a lesson in honesty. Her contributions made possible the improvement of the road leading from Concord to Pleasant View, which was a benefit to the community. She also gave generously for charitable purposes through duly recognized channels.

Before going to Concord, Mrs. Eddy had set aside a certain time in her day for driving. She strictly adhered to this arrangement, planned as a refreshing interlude. As she drove along the valley she occasionally passed an insane asylum where an inmate watched her closely through the gate. Mrs. Eddy did not permit this sad picture to disturb her, but let her thought rest upon him with such understanding of his divine birthright that he was fully restored. A milliner in the city, confined to her room with consumption, watching Mrs. Eddy as she drove past, saw something unusual in her face, and yearned to understand what it might be. Mrs. Eddy sensed her great need, and with the wordless power of divine deliverance touched the woman's receptive thought to instant healing. One day, some years later, when she was the guest of honor at the State Fair in Concord, Mrs. Eddy saw a man perform a high dive. After his act he came to her carriage to speak with her and received a remarkable healing from an old injury to his eye. Yes, this newcomer to Concord "neighbored well."

Mrs. Eddy was up and about her tasks as early as were the farmers in her vicinity. While they wrested a living from the soil with physical strength, she was increasing her knowledge of Life as God through mental might. The sun flooded bay windows through which she looked across well-kept lawns and flower gardens. To the rear of the house grassy meadows stretched around an artificial pond, the gift of students, and reached to the Merrimack. Her life, like the river, had flowed past the limiting confines of Bows and Tiltons and Amesburys with widening reaches.

There were walks through the grounds where the mistress often strolled unless the weather was stormy, when she used the broad, covered veranda. The fragrance of freshly cut hay, the singing of birds at dawn, the wind shaping branches into patterns against a sunset sky, the silver stillness of moonlight on the dew; so many gentle, lovely things nestled her tenderly within her gates. The flowers were never curious, the trees were never critical, the stars were never avaricious, the winds were never jealous. The stillness brooded close to help her pray.

Within the house all was in order and immaculate. Mrs. Laura Sargent, a member of the Chicago class, and Miss Clara Shannon, whom Mrs. Eddy had called to Pleasant View to assist her, kept the system of the house running smoothly, while Mr. Frye attended to business matters. Mrs. Eddy loved to go through her house, speaking to the various helpers and planning changes here and there. What satisfaction there must have been in doing as she wished in her own home after living so many years with strangers! She required perfection in the management of her household and was generous in appreciation of work well done. All who served her loved and revered her. She who taught others that Life is divine Principle was careful to practice her teachings in every detail of her living.

With the surroundings of a methodical household, living among those who devotedly served her, it was now possible for the Founder of the Christian Science denomination to prepare for the erection of the visible form of her church in Boston. Her experience with the publishing of Science and Health had taught her that human resistance to the establishment of advancing ideas is apt to precede their acceptance. She must therefore be fortified with divine assurance and wisdom in taking this step. Things that to others seemed impossible of accomplishment were feasible to her because she measured them with the strength of Christian power. She knew that human events rise and fall like drops of foam from the crest of a wave, while the deep currents of Truth, undisturbed, move the unbroken rhythm of eternity.

Christian Science services had first been held in private houses, in Mrs. Eddy's home, then in the College building, and finally in public halls in Boston. At last a site in the Back Bay section had been purchased, whereon to erect an edifice. In September, 1892, the lot was deeded to four of Mrs. Eddy's students, who became the first Christian Science Board of Directors. This Board consisted of Ira O. Knapp, William B. Johnson, Joseph S. Eastaman, and Stephen A. Chase. They held the property and funds in trust for all Christian Scientists throughout the Field, according to a Massachusetts law which warranted the holding of real estate in such manner. Neither debt nor lien upon the property was permitted. The Directors were also required to construct an edifice within five years, which was to cost not less than fifty thousand dollars. The entire responsibility of the work was to be theirs.

The method of reorganizing the Church had made it impossible for former memberships of malcontents to be revived, for the building to be used for any but religious purposes, and for the functioning of the Church to be less than universal.

On May 21, 1894, the cornerstone of the edifice was laid. Seven months later the Directors received the following letter from their Leader:

Pleasant View,
Concord, N. H., Dec. 19, 1894.

Christian Science Directors—
My beloved Students,

The day is well nigh won. You will soon rest on your arms. Thank God you have been valient soldiers—loyal to the heart's core. "Who is so great a God as our God"

Present no contribution box on Dedication day. When you know the amount requisite and have received it for finishing the church building—close all contributions and give public notice thereof.

Hold your services in the Mother Church Dec. 30, 1894, and dedicate this church Jan. 6th. The Bible and "Science and

Health with Key to the Scriptures" shall henceforth be the Pastor of the Mother Church. This will tend to spiritualize thought. Personal preaching has more or less of human views grafted into it. Whereas the pure Word contains only the living healthgiving Truth.

With love mother,
Mary Baker Eddy.

The edifice was completed on the date set by Mrs. Eddy. The Mother Church, The First Church of Christ, Scientist, in Boston, Massachusetts, had been erected through the spiritual conviction of Mary Baker Eddy and the gratitude and labor of a host of those whom the revelation of Christian Science had liberated from disease, sin, and even death.

Newspapers throughout the United States wrote editorially of this momentous occasion. They described the beautiful New Hampshire granite of which the church was built. They stated that the membership exceeded four thousand, and that the building had cost a quarter of a million dollars. There were also detailed descriptions of the stained-glass windows. But these things were only the shadow of the real, spiritual structure of Truth and Love. The numbers of attendants were far less significant than the fact that they had been healed of ills of the flesh through spiritual means.

And where was she whose transcendent thinking and living had given birth to this achievement? Not on the rostrum to be seen of men, not interjecting herself between her followers and their homage to Deity. Alone with God, she was working, praying, lest any sense of popularity or pride should tempt her people. Not her personal presence, but Mind's great achievement, awaited those who attended the dedicatory services in the new edifice. Personal preaching was abolished in The Mother Church, and the Bible and "Science and Health with Key to the Scriptures" were substituted as the Pastor. This necessitated the forming of Lesson-Sermons compiled from Biblical passages with correlative references from Science and Health. Another underpinning which might have continued to rest upon personal sense had been removed, and the foundation of the organization was firmly based upon divine Principle.

Now the pattern of the mount of revelation was appearing. Now the reason for the Leader's constant study of the Scriptures and revisions of the textbook was made plain. Now the utility of the By-Laws in the Church Manual was unmistakable. The truth taught in the Scriptures, and in Science and Health as their key, was to stand forever as the basis for teaching, healing, and preaching in Christian Science and for the government of the Church. The Manual rules provided for the safeguarding of this plan, preventing the possibility of personal superiority or control in any part of the structure of the movement.

In similar vein the prophet Nehemiah wrote of the Word of God reaching the people, "So they read in the book in the law of God distinctly, and gave the sense, and caused them to understand the reading." The inspired Word of the Bible was to reach the listeners of this age with unadulterated healing power. With this master stroke Mrs. Eddy knit together revelation and presentation in a way that time could not unravel.

"Science and Health with Key to the Scriptures" could not have stood the unique test put upon it by impersonal preaching had its substance not come from the same source which inspired the Bible writers. Without satiety on the part of earnest listeners it has been read correlatively with the Bible in thousands of Christian Science churches twice weekly and, like the Bible, grows more inspiring through the years.

Six years prior to the establishment of the impersonal preaching, arrangements had been made for a week-night service in which was given opportunity for those attending to testify to individual healings. This plan finally eventuated in the regular Wednesday evening meetings. Such meetings continue to furnish endless fresh evidence to the seeker of the redemptive power of Christian Science.

Not until three months after the completion of the Church edifice did Mrs. Eddy cross its threshold. On April first of that year she spent the night in the room prepared for her in the tower of the Church. Seeing her "prayer in stone" (Miscellaneous Writings, p. 141) for the first time, she asked to have the auditorium lighted. In enveloping humility she knelt on the steps of the platform in silent prayer. Then mounting the dais she repeated the ninety-first Psalm and the familiar hymn:

Guide me, O Thou great Jehovah!
  Pilgrim through this barren land:
I am weak, but Thou art mighty,
  Hold me with Thy powerful hand.
    Bread of heaven!
  Feed me till I want no more.

Open is the crystal fountain,
  Whence the healing waters flow:
And the fiery cloudy pillar
  Leads me all my journey through.
    Strong Deliverer!
  Still Thou art my strength and shield.

—*William Williams*

XVII

Church Affairs

HE nineteenth century was drawing to a close. This century had developed in the New World a young and healthy nation purged of many corrupt elements through periods of war and reconstruction. During these hundred years New England had cradled men and women of courage, wisdom, and achievement. She had seen her patriots and pioneers, her statesmen and preachers, writers, inventors, artisans, and farmers, help to weave the States into increasing unity and richness of life. She had helped the national government move on through treacherous waters of immaturity and experiment to shores of established democracy.

During these years the age of invention dawned and, as it developed, led men into further liberties. The first long-distance telephone line was constructed. The original message sent over the wires was, "What hath God wrought?" That message sounded the keynote of the century for this land.

Underneath the varied activities of the vast commonwealth ran the stratum of divine worship. Yet the period was not entirely one of men's reaching out for divine help. It was also a time when supreme reality was compelling humanity to exchange blind belief for knowledge and utilization of spiritual power. Before another half century passed, this power was to be recognized as vital for the continuance of the human race. A world struggle was to be precipitated, not only between races and nations, but between Christianity and paganism, at home and abroad. As the United States had learned that her structure could not endure so long as serfdom persisted within her borders, so the world was to become aware that it could no longer progress "half slave and half free."

Whereas physical combat had been the great deciding factor in the national struggle of the Civil War, other elements were to be essential for victory in the battle of the globe. Armies and navies, strong with inventions, wealth, and manhood, were to pour out of North America to the East and to the West, to the North and to the South, speeding to the farthest corners of the earth to defend the rights of physical and mental freedom. But this was not to be enough.

Among the weapons of humanity's foe in the years to come were to be types with which armaments would be helpless to contend. The subtlest phases of carnality were to reign for a season. To conquer such as these would be the business of Christianity, and would the followers of Christ be ready to meet the challenge? The time was coming when the Church quiescent must not only become the Church militant but the Church Triumphant, or else surrender its claim of spiritual sovereignty.

With the ending of the nineteenth century Mrs. Eddy had become a world figure. Henceforth, to the end of her earthly days, her universal-mindedness was to influence far-reaching events. At this time she wrote:

> This closing century, and its successors, will make strong claims on religion, and demand that the inspired Scriptural commands be fulfilled. The altitude of Christianity openeth, high above the so-called laws of matter, a door that no man can shut; it showeth to all peoples the way of escape from sin, disease, and death. (Christian Science *versus* Pantheism, p. 12.)

With Mrs. Eddy, foreseeing was foreknowing. Perpetual recourse to divine intelligence was increasingly natural to her. This accounts for her firm decisions and unwavering actions. Whenever the answer came to affirmative prayer she acted without hesitation. She followed Jesus' example, "whose humble prayers were deep and conscientious protests of Truth,—of man's likeness to God and of man's unity with Truth and Love" (Science and Health, p. 12). Mental pioneer that she always was, she dealt courageously with the ragged edges of human thought, where hope and faith meet with marauding fears, and was ever led into safety of realization and calm conviction. Awareness of the "strong claims" that were to be made on religion meant preparation to meet them, strengthening of work already done and new strategic positions to be taken.

With the coming of Christian Science the Christ-power advanced a hundredfold in human perception from the Christianity of creeds to the Christianity of Christ. The ceaseless vigilance, persistence, and patience of the Discoverer and Founder of Christian Science contributed to the wider development of this timely teaching. With loving care she now watched over the functioning of her Church which needed strengthening.

The Christian Science Journal, still the only official organ of The Mother Church, reached the Field but once a month. This did not provide sufficient contact between the activating center of the movement and its swiftly expanding circumference. For this reason in 1898 the *Christian Science Weekly,* soon to be named the *Christian Science Sentinel,* appeared. Mrs. Eddy closely supervised this new link between herself, her Church, and her followers. Day and night, when rest seemed already reduced to a minimum, time and attention were unstintingly given to close supervision of the new periodical to which she was a frequent contributor.

Uniform Lesson-Sermons to be read in all the Christian Science churches became indispensable. Between 1888 and 1889 there had been "Bible-Lessons" printed in the *Journal* which threw the light of Christian Science upon the International Sunday School Lessons used by Protestant churches. Gradually these Lessons used in the Christian Science churches became entirely separated from the International Lessons. They were finally composed of references from the Bible and correlative passages from Science and Health.

The twenty-six subjects of these Lesson-Sermons remain as Mrs. Eddy chose them and are repeated twice a year. They are used in the following order: "God," "Sacrament," "Life," "Truth," "Love," "Spirit," "Soul," "Mind," "Christ Jesus," "Man," "Substance," "Matter," "Reality," "Unreality," "Are Sin, Disease, and Death Real?" "Doctrine of Atonement," "Probation after Death," "Everlasting Punishment," "Adam and Fallen Man," "Mortals and Immortals," "Soul and Body," "Ancient and Modern Necromancy, *alias* Mesmerism and Hypnotism, Denounced," "God the Only Cause and Creator," "God the Preserver of Man," "Is the Universe, Including Man, Evolved by Atomic Force?" "Christian Science." There is also a Lesson-Sermon for Thanksgiving Day.

The printing of Christian Science literature now needed to be carried on under the auspices of The Mother Church. Accordingly The Christian Science Publishing Society, as it now exists, was established in 1898. Two other auxiliaries added greatly to the scope of the religious work and reached their final form during the nineties. The first was the Sunday school. In 1881 the Christian Science Sunday School had been inaugurated, but was not actually founded until 1885. At first both adults and children were allowed to attend, but in 1895 Mrs. Eddy organized the Sunday School of The Mother Church, for only children and young people. From these pupils, and those in the branch churches, she expected great spiritual fruitage in the years to come.

The second auxiliary was the Reading Room, established wherever there is a Christian Science church. These Reading Rooms were the outcome of the "Free Dispensary of Christian Science Healing" started in 1887. This work was continued later in rooms opened at 7 Temple Street, in Boston, where Bible classes, evening conversations, addresses, and the answering of questions about Christian Science healing were carried on. Patients were treated and literature was distributed. In 1894 the Christian Science Reading Rooms became a permanent part of the church work. They are now found around the world—quiet, harmonious places where countless thousands study the Bible, the works of Mrs. Eddy, and the periodicals and pamphlets of The Christian Science Publishing Society.

This ordering of the affairs of the great movement showed insight concerning the immediate and future religious needs of men. Well did the Founder of Christian Science realize that the vision of Truth would be of slight avail without adequate and acceptable presentation to the people. Divine wisdom welded into one the revelation, her love for humanity, and her perspicacity, until no weak place was left in the structure of the movement.

With this strengthening of her work, Mrs. Eddy advanced to new strategic positions, which were threefold. First, provision must be made for carrying the message of Christian Science to the general public as yet ignorant or misinformed regarding it. From pulpits and newspapers, from tongues and pens, opposition to Christian Science still persisted. Regrettable misrepresentations were made of its teachings and falsehoods spread about its Founder. To leave these mistakes uncorrected would be unfair both to Christian Science and to those misinformed concerning this religion. At this point the Board of Lectureship was initiated by the Leader.

This Board at the outset consisted of five men, whose duty it was to present Christian Science to the public in a clear and dignified manner. They were required to meet the general thought, sympathetic or otherwise, with the same spirit of patient tolerance and genuine love which their Leader had always shown in meeting the quips and questions of outsiders. These, and subsequently appointed lecturers, finally girdled the continents, lecturing in Dutch, French, German, Italian, and Spanish, as well as in English.

Secondly, more teachers were needed for the rapidly increasing number of adherents to the Cause. The Charter of the Massachusetts Metaphysical College had been retained when the College was closed. The work of preparing teachers was again made possible by the establishment of a Board of Education as an auxiliary to the Massachusetts Metaphysical College. The perpetuity and prosperity of this activity are assured, not because of largess of endowments resulting in stately buildings and renowned chairs of learning, but because of ever-widening circles of spiritually enlightened lives.

Thirdly, Mrs. Eddy established a Committee on Publication to attend to requests for information about her mission and to correct misinformation. In moving to Concord she had sought privacy wherein to accomplish work which she alone could do for the Cause. The spreading of Christian Science was of paramount concern to her. She preferred to be excused from personal interviews. Yet she was constantly becoming of more interest to the world. Here was a unique reformer who laid her "whole weight of thought, tongue, and pen in the divine scale of being—for health and holiness" (Miscellany, p. 146).

Following the appointment of the Committee on Publication for The Mother Church, the time came when there were Committees in every state, as well as in every land where the Christian Science organization became established. These "minute men" were chosen to correct impositions on the public in regard to Christian Science, as well as injustices done Mrs. Eddy, or church members, by the press or in any circulated literature.

Supervision of the interlaced activities of the rapidly expanding movement would have been more than could be compassed by a person of nearly eighty years of age, but for the fact that her strength and wisdom were drawn from the one exhaustless source, Spirit. And these activities were only a part of what Mrs. Eddy was accomplishing. The spiritual character of her work was ever the primary factor with her; never to think at variance with divine Love, never to call evil good, never to excuse error, never to act contrary to her sense of supreme guidance, never to shrink from the demands of Principle.

While co-ordinating and adding to the phases of the church work, Mrs. Eddy was ever intent upon spiritually enriching her followers. If this were thoroughly done, the Cause would stand. With this aim uppermost in thought, Mrs. Eddy once more considered teaching in response to importunate requests following the publishing of "Miscellaneous Writings." Yielding to this demand in November, 1898, she taught her last class. At her invitation the students from various countries met in Concord Christian Science Hall. There were only two sessions of this class, but how memorable they were! The first session lasted two hours and the second four hours. The vigor of her spirituality was evident to all. Her every word was rendered more effective by her own embodiment of that which she taught.

As in former classes, this uplifted teacher emphasized God's allness, the all-pervading presence of infinite good, and from this premise reiterated the unreality of evil. She taught that spiritual man is ever the complete expression of God. She counseled her pupils not to be baffled by difficult cases but to be persistent and victorious with Truth. And she adjured them to live Christian Science with humility.

Not only the letter but the spirit of Truth was poured out to the eager listeners in Mrs. Eddy's last class. Their teacher's perception had grown still keener with the passing years. Experience had enriched her with lessons dearly learned. Graciousness, strength, humor, tenderness, and insight entered into her pedagogy which was adorned with spiritual vision. Of her teaching in an earlier Normal class a pupil wrote: "We have finished our course. . . . Mrs. Eddy's teachings are beyond anything I have ever listened to. . . . It seemed as though the windows of heaven were opened and the light poured in upon us as she talked to us." (Letter by Mrs. Annie Rogers Michael.)

After more than thirty years of religious pioneering, the same serenity rested upon the teacher's brow as when she had instructed her first student. The same sweet firmness was about the mouth; the same actual seeing of the "kingdom come" shone in her eyes. The glory of her spiritual nobility gave the flush of health to her cheeks, ease to her movements, and impressiveness to her speech. It was evident that her ministry had not been a human struggle against overwhelming odds, but a steadfast moving with divine omnipotence.

The Christian Science Church in Boston had become the mother-vine of a constantly increasing number of branches. The reinstatement of primitive Christian healing was flourishing in the movement and being attempted in other denominations. Means of protecting the purity of this teaching and practice were established. Respect for Christian Science was taking the place of ridicule and misunderstanding. With quiet step, and yet with a cloak of wonder that would not let it pass unnoticed, religion was spreading the Science of Christ, redemption from every form of evil upon the earth. The nineteenth century was giving to the twentieth a resplendent heritage.

"What hath God wrought?"

XVIII

Opposition Overcome

OR many years Mrs. Eddy had been loving the human race and laboring incessantly for world emancipation from false beliefs. Humanity was feeling the effect of the alterative power of Christian Science. Wherever the truth of being reached receptive thought, there liberation from some discordant sense took place and the ranks of spiritually aroused thinkers were increased. Where it touched the darkness of evil in caverns of the human mind, it stirred resistance. But the revelation of the Science of Life had come to deliver all men from self-imposed bondage, whether they would or not. Its universal course was set, its strength exhaustless. No human hand had released its mighty loving, and none could stay it.

It was inevitable that both the gratitude of the receptive and the enmity of the resistant should be directed to that quiet home in Concord where the herald of the new religious era dwelt. It was well that Christian Science had not come to wage a defensive warfare against evil, but to reveal the divine facts of

Life to men. Thus spiritual history would repeat itself, for "Jesus stormed sin in its citadels and kept peace with God" (Miscellaneous Writings, p. 211).

On rare occasions, Mrs. Eddy permitted her followers to come to her home. She had addressed them in The Mother Church, and once in Tremont Temple when she left the meeting before adjournment in order that she might avoid a reception. The first time she acted as hostess to these eager friends under her own roof about two hundred came. She welcomed them cordially, gave them the freedom of the house, and talked with them all. Two years later about twenty-five hundred came and her greeting to them was in the form of an address. Then refreshments were served on the lawn. Three other times large groups went to Pleasant View after the Communion service in Boston. Special trains were provided for them. On the occasion of the last gathering, in 1903, about ten thousand people assembled on the spacious grounds.

Long before this, Mrs. Eddy had become a public personage, but to the members of her Church she was more than ever their spiritual guide, God's messenger to mankind, one whom they loved with reverence. As they gathered for the last time on the lawn at Pleasant View they quietly awaited their Leader's greeting. Speechless joy and breathless anticipation surged over the crowd as a graceful form appeared on the balcony and Mrs. Eddy, advancing to the rail, stood looking out upon them all, her hands extended with palms upraised. The gesture was one of welcome and benediction. In her movement there was no ecclesiastical attitude, no touch of personal authority. The widespread palms spoke eloquently of receptivity and generosity. It was as though she said, as did the Master, "All mine are thine, and thine are mine" (John 17:10).

The light of ceaseless communion with the living God, utter devotion to her trust, the scope of her spiritual journeying, and the indescribable love which embraced those upon whom her thought rested, were visible in her face. Conquerings softened with the peace of overcoming were there. The whole figure spoke of the yielding of the human to the divine.

And what did this humble Leader of a mighty movement see in the crowd of upturned faces? Doubtlessly the fruit of endless prayer and work, the healed of the Lord, the confirmation of hope, the proof of the axioms of Christian Science, the sign of the "kingdom come," the dawn of universal redemption. Briefly, Mrs. Eddy spoke to the silent throng, her voice reaching to the farthest listener.

Once more members of her Church were to hear her when, in the following year, about two thousand attended the dedication of First Church of Christ, Scientist, in Concord, Mrs. Eddy's gift to her pupils in that city. On this occasion she spoke from her carriage, which drew up in front of the edifice.

This mental pioneer of the unknown realm of Spirit had accomplished mighty tasks. Her justly earned laurels were many, her name known on every continent. Might it not be that the days of exploration were over and the time of homing come? Could not the busy hands drop the pen and rest a little while? Could not the pressing hours slip by more gently? Just a short release from endless demands would have seemed a fair request to make. But this respite was not for her. Instead, amazing unfoldment of Science work was becoming clarified in her consciousness, soon to be translated into action. Bitter enmity was also preparing to deal her and her work a severe blow which later proved but a boomerang to the perpetrator.

This blow came in a series of lawsuits begun in 1899. They were brought against Mrs. Eddy and others in Boston by one who had been expelled from membership in The Mother Church several years before. This unjust attack was conducted in a sensational way, and at the end of two years one of the suits reached the courts. The verdict was rendered in Mrs. Eddy's favor. She endured this experience with quiet fortitude. The trial did not prevent her usual activities. She knew better than to step aside from the highway of her labors as error passed, leaving her unscathed and her Cause unharmed.

During this period Mrs. Eddy once said: "Work has grown to be a habit with me. There is much to be done; and our desire is to do so much in a short time." (*Christian Science Sentinel,* September 13, 1900.) The unfailing energy of Life with which this Christian worked never exhausted her. There was an inner stillness about her which embraced her industry, a freshness which mellowed the touch of years, a drinking in of immortal essence which silenced the flesh.

The desire to do, and do much, was just as keen as when Mrs. Eddy first sought the Science of Christian healing. Her step was still quick upon the stairs, her thought alert to revelation, her concern for mankind unabated. Though she called workers to Pleasant View at different times to aid her with ever-mounting tasks, and though the church members were proving their own God-directed abilities to carry on the multiplying duties of the movement, the Leader took no time for leisure. The attraction of spiritual discovery never ceased to draw her. The application of her learning never reached an *outrance.* However fast the movement flourished, she was still blazing the trail ahead.

Mrs. Eddy's message to members of The Mother Church in June, 1902, read at the Annual Meeting of the Church to assemblies of about ten thousand, conveyed the writer's breadth and clarity of thought.

Thoroughly cognizant of the progressive status of the Cause, she reiterated the permanent and universal nature of Christian Science. She referred to the alterative effect of Truth upon human existence, and foretold the ultimate peace it would bring to all men. There were references to religious changes in the Orient, to the inauguration of home rule and the withdrawal of our military forces in Cuba. Allusion was also made to the close of the war in South Africa and the coronation of King Edward of England.

The message contained spiritual explanation of the First Commandment and of the Master's command "that ye love one another; as I have loved you." It showed the Christian doctrine applicable alike to Jew and Gentile, and counseled the adoption of Jesus' attitude in persecution, declaring that his followers would be triumphant over trials. There was reference to the public acceptance of telegraphy and steam power, and a pleading for like acceptance of the liberating capacities of scientific religion. Much was said regarding the ethics of Christian Science, and how to forestall and conquer discord.

The message included a recommendation to enlarge the Church edifice. This called for the purchase of more property whereon to build, and was accepted by the assembly of members. They at once committed themselves and the whole field of workers to the raising of any sum, up to two million dollars, necessary for the accomplishment of their Leader's plan. The clearing of land next to the original structure began in October, 1903. Nine months later the cornerstone was laid, and in 1906 the finished Extension of The Mother Church, free of debt, and with a seating capacity of about five thousand, lifted its great dome against the sky. Mrs. Eddy writes: "Methinks this church is the one edifice on earth which most prefigures self-abnegation, hope, faith; love catching a glimpse of glory" (Miscellany, p. 6).

The "glimpse of glory" was unmistakable at the first Wednesday evening meeting in the new auditorium. From the platform came the ringing declaration of the ever-presence of Christ-power; from the pews, the echoes of healings accomplished. Those who testified told of release from poverty, failure, discouragement, sorrow, sickness, and sin. Attestations flowed forth from untutored and from cultured lips, from former members of ministerial and medical professions, from persons of varying rank and race. Only the time for closing stopped this joyous rendering of thanks to God.

Content to abide with the substance, rather than the symbol, of Truth, the Founder of Christian Science never entered the Extension edifice. All she asked of the world was time, alone, in which "to assimilate more of the divine character" (Science and Health, p. 4), and to work for all men.

Impressive results were to follow Mrs. Eddy's wilderness days! She was realizing the slow but inevitable transition of general thought from faith in matter to the understanding of spiritual substance and Life. Being aware of the upheavals which would always accompany this change, her compassion for humanity was constantly quickened. She knew the false beliefs of mortals, their roots, branches, and fruits, as well as the laws of divine Science which were obliterating these beliefs. There was need to meet men's doubts, fears, discouragements, and even their rejection of the saving Truth. She must listen for Christian wiseness with which to meet this need. She was not only beholding, but living, divine facts, thus encouraging others to venture into the same spiritual safety.

Suddenly, the world which had tried to ignore Mary Baker Eddy now resented her aloofness. To be sure, she had responded to requests from leading newspapers and magazines for statements on moral issues and world affairs. But she evaded personal interviews and the world now wanted to know the reason. Curiosity said, "There must be something wrong." Perhaps, after all, she was a person who said one thing and did another. Intrusion said, "I will find out."

Once, in 1905, Mrs. Eddy broke her rule about interviews and received a representative of *The Boston Herald.* This reporter was so impressed with her gracious presence, her evident well-being in spite of years, and her absorption in the affairs of Spirit, that she withdrew and permitted Mrs. Eddy to answer her prepared questions by letter. This Mrs. Eddy did with appreciation of the reporter's courtesy. But instead of helping the public situation, this interview fanned curiosity's flame. In newspaper offices surmise was busy. Here was a world figure, front-page news, yet they could not get at her. Was her seclusion a clever pose to excite further interest, or a means to cover frailty? It might be that she was no longer able to attend to her business and that a substitute took the daily ride, while members of the household dominated her and her affairs. There might be sensational disclosures. This was reason enough for reporters to invade Mrs. Eddy's home and turn upon her the glaring flashlight of publicity.

In the autumn following the dedication of The Mother Church Extension two representatives of a New York daily paper came to Concord determined to stay until they secured information to substantiate preconceived errors of judgment touching the Discoverer and Founder of Christian Science. They arrived at Pleasant View in a mood which would brook no denial of their demand for a personal interview. Their aggressive demeanor disturbed the ordered household, whose members tried to spare Mrs. Eddy the ordeal of this unwarranted intrusion, but these reporters would not be satisfied until they had seen her in the flesh.

When the mistress of the home was told of the presence and attitude of these callers, she replied that she would see them, together with a neighbor who could testify to her daily life of simplicity and sincerity. When they were ushered into her study where she was writing, she felt the malice of their thoughts and flushed slightly, trembling a little as she rose to greet them. They were given time to put their questions to this gentlewoman whose eighty-five years of blameless and unselfish living merited courteous and fair treatment at their hands. But they went back to their desks to fabricate and publish a tale of decrepitude, deceit, and incapacity which shocked their readers. People in general did not believe that a person who had so greatly benefited countless sufferers could stoop to cheap trickery, or be the dupe of designing persons. The news writers of the country rejected the implications of the reported interview, and the paper which claimed a "scoop" was discredited.

Newspaperdom, however, was not satisfied to let the matter drop. Within twenty-four hours after the fabrications appeared, the Associated Press, the Publishers Press, and leading Boston and New York papers sent representatives to Concord. The Christian Science Committee on Publication sent an assistant to deal with the situation. He consulted with Mrs. Eddy's two secretaries, who proceeded to procure affidavits of Mrs. Eddy's business relations with some of the leading citizens of Concord and her social relations with those about her. Editors of the two most prominent New Hampshire papers, the president of the National State Capital Bank, the leading lawyer of the New Hampshire bar, the mayor of the city, and others gladly furnished favorable testimonials regarding their illustrious and respected townswoman. These affidavits left no doubt that it was Mrs. Eddy who went for a daily drive through the gates of Pleasant View, that she was capable of attending to her own affairs, and that she was in good health.

This array of evidence was not enough to satisfy the press. Their insistent and joint request for a personal interview with Mrs. Eddy was finally granted. In response to her invitation, about a score of newspapermen, the mayor of Concord, her banker, and her lawyer, together with a few gentlemen from The Mother Church, gathered in her drawing room just before she went for her daily drive. Down the stairway she came to be mercilessly scrutinized. But look as penetratingly as they would at the erect figure daintily gowned, at the clear eyes challenging their skepticism, and test as they might the courage of honest conviction ringing in her replies to their questions, these men found no trace of anything unfavorable. When Mrs. Eddy terminated the interview by going to her carriage, the visitors were allowed to go through the house. Their careful investigation yielded the evidence of an orderly New England home where everyone was occupied faithfully serving the Leader of a great spiritual movement, where precious moments were used for unselfish labor, and where even inspection of closets and cupboards furnished nothing upon which curiosity could feed.

After the invasive visit to Pleasant View it became evident that frustrated evil was intent upon finding a way whereby to counteract permanently the ever-growing influence of Mrs. Eddy's reformative teachings. Articles delving into her human history appeared in newspapers and magazines, and the cleverest American humorist of the times wrote a book on his impressions of Christian Science which unmercifully ridiculed this religion and its Discoverer, yet acknowledged as still animate the Christian requirement to heal the sick and sinning by spiritual means. But the agency through which the first attack had been launched against Mrs. Eddy's probity found an avenue through which to deal a direct blow.

The nefarious scheme was to bring a suit against Mrs. Eddy and others close to her, charging mental incapacity and domination of her person and her affairs by associates. To this end two New York newspapers ferreted out Mrs. Eddy's son, George Glover, in Lead City, South Dakota, a nephew, George W. Baker, in Maine, and her adopted son, Dr. E. J. Foster-Eddy. These men were persuaded that something was vitally wrong with the management of their relative's valuable estate, and that it was their duty to take possession of the estate for Mrs. Eddy's benefit. Under the guise of benevolence a suit was brought into court which could have stripped Mrs. Eddy of her right to use her earnings as she desired, affected her copyrights, and taken from her the freedom to carry forward her vast achievement.

Again and again Mary Baker Eddy had risen to the defense of the Cause of Christian Science. This time more than ever before she needed to "abide under the shadow of the Almighty." The assault was deadly, but the power upon which she leaned for wisdom and strength was omniscient and omnipotent. She immediately created a trusteeship, transferring all her property, and the care of it under certain conditions, to three men: her cousin, her banker, and a member of The Christian Science Board of Directors, who was also editor of *The Christian Science Journal* and *Sentinel.* In preparation for this step she had already created a trust deed to provide liberally for her son and his family. Thereby funds for the education of the children were assured.

The plaintiffs had an eminent array of counsel, but the first part of the case was dismissed at once. They then tried to bring Mrs. Eddy into court. Finally the court appointed three masters to wait upon her to take her testimony. They came by appointment to Pleasant View on August 14, 1907, together with the senior counsel on each side. This unusual courtesy was extended to Mrs. Eddy by the Honorable Edgar Aldrich, who was constituted master of the court to hear the evidence and to determine the defendant's condition. The other two masters were the eminent alienist, Dr.

George F. Jelly of Boston, and the Honorable Hosea W. Parker, a distinguished lawyer of Claremont, New Hampshire.

Unusual importunity brought this group to a New England home to try the mental capacity of the outstanding religious Leader of the day. Their impressions might form an adverse decision that could impair the work of a lifetime, affect the faith of thousands, and spiritually as well as financially impoverish a great Cause. This judicial body, sitting in judgment upon a woman acknowledged by a world-wide following as one of God's messengers, was trying more than a suit at law. The decision was to be formed by a higher jurisdiction than theirs.

Mrs. Eddy, calm and confident, was ready for the ordeal. A member of her household came part way with her to the study where she was to receive her examiners; then she went on alone. Before reaching the door she waited a few seconds, then continued. Mrs. Eddy's companion was distressed lest an impression of hesitancy, indecision, or weakness had been given which would be detrimental to the defendant.

Mrs. Eddy received her guests with courteous dignity and answered their questions with such acumen that there was no doubt left in their minds as to her business ability, her civic interests, or her harmonious relations with members of her household. When the examination ceased it was evident to the opposing counsel that the masters' findings would be in favor of the defendant, and he determined to withdraw the suit. When the visitors had left the house, Mrs. Eddy's companion hurried to her and burst out with the question, "Why did you hesitate before entering the room?" Instantly the answer came, "I was waiting for the Christ to go before me."

Some years later, one of the masters spoke about Mrs. Eddy in a most tender way to two Christian Scientists. He said that he had been one of the number sent by the court to examine her at the time of the "Next Friends" suit. He spoke of his prejudice against her until their meeting that day, when he recognized that she was one of the most intelligent women he had ever met, and also the most spiritual. In a short time the three masters were of one mind in their favorable attitude toward her. As with her childhood fever induced by the harshness of false theology, so with this phase of aggression in her later years, Mary Baker Eddy experienced the power of divine deliverance.

The "Next Friends" suit collapsed. All that it had achieved was the clarifying of public opinion regarding Mrs. Eddy. The decision received almost unanimous press approval. At Mrs. Eddy's instigation a costly book on the suit was withdrawn from publication, lest it preserve a spirit of enmity against those who had attacked her. She generously reimbursed the Concord editor who had prepared the record. Her loving was too deep and broad to be crushed, or to become self-centered. Its fragrance still went abroad. Without pause, this ardent pilgrim turned to preparation of another great enterprise.

XIX

Further Achievement

OR sixteen years Mrs. Eddy had lifted her eyes to the hills beyond her peaceful acres as she worked, prayed, and sought the direction of the creator of the universe. With the coming of the year 1908 it became apparent that Concord was too remote from Boston for her to maintain essential contacts with the functionaries of the Church. There was a great undertaking in view, with added demands upon all concerned.

Putting the demands of the Cause before any human disinclination to leave the countryside with its accustomed pathways and established comforts, on January 26 Mrs. Eddy moved to a spacious stone residence surrounded by twelve acres of land in Chestnut Hill, a suburb of Boston. The new house, with its twenty-five rooms, was well adapted to a growing staff of helpers. It had been purchased by the Trustees some time previously, and completely furnished.

The weather on the day of the journey was delightful for the time of year. A few Christian Scientists and her nearest relative at hand accompanied Mrs. Eddy.

She mounted the steps of the special train with vivacity and was keenly interested in every phase of the trip. When they arrived at Chestnut Hill some newspapermen who had been notified that Mrs. Eddy had left Concord had gathered in front of the house. A member of her party, seeing the curious onlookers, assisted her in evading their intrusion. When she reached the upper hall she laughed heartily over the episode. She had seen enough of reporters for a while.

When it became known in Concord that the city had lost its most prominent citizen, there was widespread regret. Mrs. Eddy was highly esteemed by the community in which she had lived so long. Many loved her for neighborly acts. Her residence in Concord resulted in many civic improvements and donations to the city. But more than any other gift, the atmosphere of her religious life and teaching blessed the city of her choice.

The City Council met and passed resolutions of appreciation of her stay in their midst, and regret at her leaving. The mayor and clerk were authorized to convey these sentiments to her. In replying, Mrs. Eddy wrote of valuing their expressions of kindness and ended with this paragraph:

My home influence, early education, and church experience, have unquestionably ripened into the fruits of my present religious experience, and for this I prize them. May I honor this origin and deserve the continued friendship and esteem of the people in my native State.

Sincerely yours,

Mary Baker G. Eddy.

(The Life of Mary Baker Eddy, by Sibyl Wilbur, p. 356.)

A few hours after her arrival at Chestnut Hill, Mrs. Eddy slipped into her routine work. Occasionally there was a resting hour in the afternoon, but there were times at night when her thoughts and pen were active. With explanation, correction, and example she helped those about her to progress in scientific knowing and living. She was joyous in all that she did. Her contemplation of things immortal was vital in expression. Never had she seemed more spiritually strong. At this time divine energy was impelling her toward a considerable undertaking, one which had been developing in her thought for over twenty years.

The time was not far distant when the age of living on the surface of land and sea would merge into an age of existence beneath the waters and above the earth. Expanding liberties of thought and action would demand further understanding of God's laws which reach to the clouds and are enforced in the depths. Man's sense of home was gradually to be enlarged from a city to a world; his sense of brotherhood, from a human family to all mankind; his sense of movement, from plodding to soaring. Mrs. Eddy foresaw this progress, not as cycles of material development, but as the gradual reappearing of the primitive, eternal truth of man and the universe.

This mental pioneer was aware that "the evolutions of advancing thought" (Miscellaneous Writings, pp. 1, 2) would require a suitable medium of expression. A daily newspaper whose whole policy was "to injure no man, but to bless all mankind" (Miscellany, p. 353), whose viewpoint was universal, whose purpose was to assist the passage of human thought from material groping to spiritual knowing, would serve this scientific purpose. Through such a daily paper the awakening of the world to eternal facts would be speeded. The quality of the news would be more than reported, it would be unfolded.

Through those first spring months at Chestnut Hill, Mary Baker Eddy prepared to inaugurate an international daily newspaper. She drank in much of divine wisdom before making her plan known to others. Then, her thought was clear, her decision considered, her step certain.

On August 8, 1908, she wrote to the Board of Trustees:

It is my request that you start a daily newspaper at once, and call it *The Christian Science Monitor*. Let there be no delay. The Cause demands that it be issued now.

You may consult with the Board of Directors, I have notified them of my intention.

In the *Christian Science Sentinel* of October 17, 1908, the following extract appeared in an editorial:

With the approval of our Leader, Mrs. Eddy, The Christian Science Publishing Society will shortly issue a daily newspaper to be known as *The Christian Science Monitor*. In making this announcement we can say for the Trustees of the Society that they confidently hope and expect to make the *Monitor* a worthy addition to the list of publications issued by the Society. It is their intention to publish a strictly up-to-date newspaper, in which all the news of the day that should be printed will find a place, and whose service will not be restricted to any one locality or section, but will cover the daily activities of the entire world. . . .

It will be the mission of the *Monitor* to publish the real news of the world in a clean, wholesome manner, devoid of the sensational methods employed by so many newspapers. There will be no exploitation or illustration of vice and crime, but the aim of the editors will be to issue a paper which will be welcomed in every home where purity and refinement are cherished ideals.

As soon as the first request for funds reached the Christian Science field, contributions began to pour into the Publishing Society. These continued until the amount was sufficient to purchase more land, to build an addition to the Publishing House, and to buy new printing presses. The work went forward with persistence until, on November 25, 1908, the day before Thanksgiving, the first issue of the paper appeared, a Thanksgiving herald to the world. Within three months the land had been purchased and cleared of buildings; arrangements had been made for former tenants; offices had been built and equipped; the staff assembled, and the first issue of the daily published. Mrs. Eddy was closely in touch with all the work and guided the policy of the paper after it had been launched.

Some were dubious about the use of the words "Christian Science" in the title of the paper, even to the point of discussing the matter with Mrs. Eddy. She was unyielding and time has proved that she knew best. She wrote of these words: "The two largest words in the vocabulary of thought are 'Christian' and 'Science.' The former is the highest style of man; the latter reveals and interprets God and man; it aggregates, amplifies, unfolds, and expresses the ALL-God." (No and Yes, p. 10.)

Gradually, *The Christian Science Monitor* has made its way beyond the ranks of Christian Scientists. It is to be found in bookstalls, schools, legislative halls, and libraries, in hotels, on ships, and in embassies. It has the respect and admiration of its associates, the appreciation of great statesmen, of business and professional men on both sides of the Atlantic and Pacific. With background of scientific religion, with respect for truth in the deepest meaning of the word, it publishes the falsity of evil and the reality of good. It is slowly drawing the weight of thought to the side of the commendable, the moral. It continues contributing notably to international harmony and world progress, so notably that it has been the first newspaper to receive honors and a medal for furthering international understanding. *The Christian Science Monitor* already fulfills its Founder's intention in a large degree.

In the course of the two years which followed the appearing of *The Christian Science Monitor,* Mrs. Eddy's mortal sense of existence was drawing to a close. Eternal being was constantly growing clearer to her. Time was found for deeper study and for prayer fresh with new views of divine Love. There were communications to officials on church matters. There was also deep interest in the growth of Christian Science in the Old World. Churches were now functioning in England, Scotland, and in Germany.

Such hopes fulfilled, such achievement to rejoice in, such fruitage still in seed! Though loved by multitudes, Mrs. Eddy loved more than all. Though served by willing hands, her own served the Master better. Though Leader of a widespread movement, none was so led as she. The light of revelation shining through her clear consciousness was enlightening the world.

The days went by with orderly activity. Reports from the movement came to her desk where decisions were made and counsel given. Occasionally Mrs. Eddy's household joined her in singing old songs and loved hymns. Greatly prized were the periods of study of the Bible and Science and Health, with inspiration shared with those around her.

December, 1910, arrived. On the first day of the month Mrs. Eddy took her drive as usual and rested after her return. She then called for a pad and pencil and wrote the words, "God is my life." The following day she was about and talked to her household gathered in her study. On the evening of December 3, quietly, bravely, alone, she walked "through the valley of the shadow" to journey on in Life immeasurable.

XX

God's Messenger

HE afterglow of Mary Baker Eddy's lifework spreads across the earth, embracing multitudes in its wonder and its mercy. So firmly did the great Leader found the Christian Science movement on divine Principle that prophecy of the passing of the revelation of Christian Science with her going was unfulfilled. Her followers, as a whole, remained undisturbed, quickened with a deeper sense of responsibility. She had ever turned the devotion of her people Godward.

Several years after the passing of its Founder, the Christian Science organization survived a severe testing period. The Board of Trustees of The Christian Science Publishing Society function under a Deed of Trust executed by Mrs. Eddy in 1898, as stated in the Manual of The Mother Church. Each member of the Board accepts the Trust before assuming office. In 1919, disaffected Trustees of the Publishing Society endeavored to separate the publishing business from The Mother Church, contesting the right of the Board of Directors to supervise their work and to remove a

Trustee. At this time a dismissed member of The Christian Science Board of Directors started litigation for the purpose of being reinstated. These activities challenged provisions in the Church Manual. The suits continued for two years, but the Supreme Judicial Court of Massachusetts, in its decision, upheld Mrs. Eddy's form of organization. The laws of the land vindicated and left intact the institution of the Christian Science Cause. Mrs. Eddy once stated that the Church Manual would be "acknowledged as law by law" (Historical Sketches, by Clifford P. Smith, p. 220).

About a decade later the Christian Science field contributed the sum of over four million dollars for the erection of a new Publishing House adequate for the substantial growth of Christian Science in this and other lands. This seemed miraculous to onlookers, as had the building of the original edifice of The Mother Church in 1894, for each accomplishment had been carried to completion during a time of nation-wide financial depression.

In the Publishing House is a Mapparium, a unique, spherical room, depicting the map of the world in colored glass. Here the thoughtful observer may trace the spread of Christian Science activities and envisage what future journeyings await the teachings of her who lived to bring Christian healing to all mankind.

German, French, and Braille editions of the textbook are now in circulation. Other published writings by Mrs. Eddy are translated into several different languages. *The Herald of Christian Science* is published monthly in French and German; a Scandinavian edition with an equal number of articles in Danish, Norwegian, and Swedish, a Dutch edition, a Spanish edition, and a Braille edition, are published quarterly. Pamphlets are printed in many languages, as are also religious articles in *The Christian Science Monitor.*

The transcendent ideas revealed through Mrs. Eddy's writings will eventually deliver the peoples of all nations wearily groping their way out of far-spent materialism. So great an accomplishment could not be nourished by the shallow stream of human ambition. The revelation of Christian Science springs from the waters of eternal Life.

The history of Christianity, stained with blood and bitterness since the days of Bethlehem's star, found in Mary Baker Eddy the agency fitted to reflect again the motherhood of God so wonderfully exemplified in the healing might of Christ Jesus. Mrs. Eddy talked with God and showed to men the way of heaven that does not pass through hell. Hers was profound insight into the nature of divine Love, a vast advance in the universal struggle for health, holiness, and freedom.

She passed through deep valleys of searching to high peaks of vision. There were times when hatred stoned the spirit of this pilgrim, but left it resurgent; times when intolerance shot its arrows, but there was no resentment to barb them. There were times when opposition stormed against a courage mailed with divine omnipotence. Without pause, without haste, she kept the upward way until her goal was reached.

Mrs. Eddy sought and found the things that cannot be shaken. She learned the power of infinite Love. She adapted this power to humanity's ills and saw it conquer mortal sins and torments. Through her discovery the putting off of mortality and the putting on of immortality took on a definite pattern which all can follow. In other words, she gave the world comprehension of Christian healing and its Science of redemption.

Her spiritual daring challenged the hosts of evil. With boldness of Spirit, the Christian Science Leader flung her battle line across the length, depth, and breadth of material belief and never retreated from this position. With keen insight she conquered every phase of evil through spiritual understanding. Her revelation of God's allness disproved sin's pretense of reality and the presumption of sickness. It stripped from death its camouflage of sanctity. It wakened human beings from the sleep-walking of mortality to the vitality of eternal Life.

Mrs. Eddy's spiritual warfare was waged for the liberation of all men from slavery to materialism. Though at times timid, and by nature modest and retiring, she wrestled with the flesh, evil, and the world, and prevailed. Her warfare did not weary her, pessimism did not lay hold upon her. She finished her course with joy and made her years on earth an anthem of praise to God. When triumphs came, she who sought His approval needed and asked no honor of men. Fitted to her lips could have been the song of Samuel: "Thou hast also given me the shield of thy salvation: and thy gentleness hath made me great" (II Samuel 22:36).

This student of the infinite beheld the all-embracing aspect of divine Love. She felt its ever-presence. She saw man's inseparability from Love. She demonstrated Love's dominion through divine healing, so that men felt the tender, compassionate, controlling touch of the Principle of the universe. Time will turn the pages of her life's message and civilization will read its wonder in progressive Christendom.

Mrs. Eddy rose to leadership of multitudes through inspired thought. She carried her followers with her, not as faddists, but as adherents of Biblical truths. In religious and medical circles the divinely inspired doctrine of Christian Science affects the views of many who have not adopted her teachings. Through scientific revelation, not mystical imagination, she opened to humanity the realm of the unseen, and substantiated her claims with healing works.

Mrs. Eddy's words and works are a living urge to the followers of Christian Science, as to all Christians, to understand better the full meaning of Christ Jesus' mission on earth. Her Christian success grew from her implicit obedience to what she discerned in Scripture as the word of God. There is need for Christian Scientists constantly to rededicate themselves to similar obedience and to the solemn task of Christian healing, so that the Discoverer of divine Science shall not have lived in vain.

The Christian Science Church continues to function and expand, reflecting in ever-increasing degree the Church Universal and Triumphant. Stripped of pretentious ceremonial, virile, and unhampered by creed, rich with proof of divine power, it goes its way, gathering beneath its wings those in need of healing and redemption. The intangible structure of rebuilt lives, the temple not made with hands, still rises higher and higher.

Mrs. Eddy lived in the nineteenth century, but her thought embraced all centuries. Rising above the mists of age-old beliefs, she reached the threshold of eternal facts. The awesome grandeur of her discovery enveloped her and carried her through arduous years of ministry. This discovery revived the language of Spirit, restored the recognition of divine presence, and revealed the eternal Science of man's being.

This Science shows man to be spiritual, the forever likeness of God; man, against whom no weapon that is formed can prosper; man, who knows no liaison with evil; man, whose being is immortality. As Thomas Moore succinctly puts it:

> And from the lips of Truth one mighty breath
> Shall, like a whirlwind, scatter in its breeze
> That whole dark pile of human mockeries;
> Then shall the reign of Mind commence on earth,
> And starting fresh, as from a second birth,
> Man in the sunshine of the world's new spring,
> Shall walk transparent, like some holy thing.

The conviction and spiritual serenity of Mrs. Eddy's writings, the conquests of her mission, the character of her followers, the soundness of her religious structure based on the life and teachings of the Master, have left a permanent impress upon human progress. The leaven of true understanding which Christian Science has put into human consciousness is cleansing it from superstition, ignorance, and slavery. It is lifting humanity to spiritual vantage ground where the waning of materialism is discerned and the reign of righteousness experienced. The work of this great friend of humanity combines divine revelation with "signs following" in a degree unprecedented since the earliest annals of the Christian church.

In the depths of her consciousness Mrs. Eddy knew that in her discovery of Christian Science was fulfilled the Bible prophecy of a woman who would bring forth a man child to rule all nations with the power of God (Revelation 12:5). Passing years are confirming her prescience with ever-increasing evidence of spiritual healing and freedom from finiteness among men.

With patience and tolerance for all, with tender compassion and healing power, with love unfeigned and impartial, with simplicity and sincerity, with vision and strength of destiny, the woman divinely foretold fulfilled her mission. She wrote in "Miscellaneous Writings" (p. 158), "As of old, I stand with sandals on and staff in hand, waiting for the watchword and the revelation of what, how, whither."